Grande Café au lait croissant
Plan de Paris par Arrondissement

CHEAP EATS in PARIS

Sandra A. Gustafson

CHRONICLE BOOKS

SAN FRANCISCO

Printed in the United States of America

Library of Congress Cataloging-in-Publication Data available.

ISBN 0-8118-0057-1

Editing: Carolyn Miller
Cover design: Robin Weiss
Cover photograph: © Dallas and John Heaton/Afterimage
Cover map: Historic Urban Plans, Ithaca, NY
Book design: Words & Deeds

Distributed in Canada by
Raincoast Books
112 East Third Avenue
Vancouver, B.C. V5T 1C8

10 9 8 7 6 5 4 3 2

Chronicle Books
275 Fifth Street
San Francisco, CA 94103

For Barbie and Marv

CONTENTS

TO THE READER

Paris is a feast, but the banquet has become painfully expensive.
— Anthony Dias Blue

Along with the Louvre, the Eiffel Tower, and the Champs-Élysées, dining *à la française* is an integral part of any successful trip to Paris. The French know how to eat; if there is something a French person would rather do, no one has yet discovered what it is. For the French, good food is not a casual interest expressed only when eating out, but a way of life and a celebration of the bounty of foods available throughout the year. As a result, French cooking has been raised to an art form and is practiced with great talent and skill. This love of good food is reflected in the more than 20,000 cafés, bistros, brasseries, and restaurants in Paris that cater to every taste and budget, from haute cuisine to hole-in-the-wall.

It is easy, if you have unlimited funds, to dine at one of the Parisian cathedrals of cuisine and to have an exquisite meal for more than $150 per person. Choosing a place to eat can be frustrating and time-consuming, because it is quite possible to eat badly and to pay too much if you don't have any guidelines. As a visitor to Paris, you don't want to waste time and money on a mediocre meal when you could be eating well and paying less just around the corner.

The purpose of *Cheap Eats in Paris* is to help you to improve the quality of your Parisian eating experiences and to save you money by leading you around that corner, away from the tourist-packed high-priced restaurants to the well-located picturesque ones that serve reasonably priced meals to mostly French patrons. *Cheap Eats in Paris* will introduce you to all types of places: crowded, noisy cafés with a haze of pungent Gauloise smoke and a coterie of colorful regulars; family-run bistros with red and white checked tablecloths, and sawdust on the floor; sophisticated wine bars; cozy tearooms; big brasseries serving steaming platters of *choucroute*; and candlelit restaurants that couples leave more in love than when they arrived. Some of these are classics everyone has heard about. Others, until now, have been unknown to foreigners. A few are Big Splurges that have been selected for special occasions for those of you who enjoy an abundance of the very best.

My research trip for this edition took me to parts of Paris I otherwise wouldn't have visited and led me to many new and exciting dining discoveries that I will share with you. In an effort to save you money and to keep you from making as many mistakes as possible, I spent eight weeks revisiting every listing in the 1990–91 edition of *Cheap Eats in Paris,* as well as trying countless others that for one reason or another did not make the final cut for this current edition. I have been seated in English-speaking Siberias near the kitchen, under the fan, and behind a post; suffered through nearly inedible meals; been overcharged by condescending waiters; sat on chairs that could have been used in the Inquisition; and received the country-bumpkin treatment from start to finish just so you can avoid doing the same thing.

Many old favorite Cheap Eats remain. Unfortunately, some tried-and-true entries from past editions have been dropped. Places that were once wonderful are now dreadful; chefs and owners have changed and prices have risen to a mind-numbing level. Cozy corner cafés have fallen victim to fast-food joints, and the age of concrete and modernization has removed others.

The result of my research is the present edition of *Cheap Eats in Paris,* with more than 150 cafés, bistros, brasseries, restaurants, tearooms, and wine bars that offer good food quality and top value for your dining franc, thus enabling you to cut corners in style.

In the back of the book is a page for your comments and notes. Naturally, I hope you are as enthusiastic about your choice of restaurants from *Cheap Eats in Paris* as I was in selecting them. I also hope *Cheap Eats* will give you the confidence to strike out on your own and to make your own discoveries. If you find someplace wonderful or you want to report a change, please take a few moments to write me a note telling me about your experiences. I follow up on every letter, and I cannot emphasize enough how important your letters and comments are.

Whether for business, sightseeing, or as a stop on the way to another destination, Paris has been beckoning travelers for hundreds of years, and most visitors have treasured memories of their stay in the City of Light. One of the best souvenirs you can have of a trip to Paris is the memory of a good meal. I hope that by using *Cheap Eats in Paris* you will have some very special memories of Paris to take home with you. *Bon voyage,* and, of course, *bon appétit!*

How to Use
Cheap Eats in Paris

Each listing in *Cheap Eats in Paris* includes the following information: the name of the establishment, the address, the arrondissement (in parentheses), the telephone number, the most convenient Métro stop, when it is open and closed, whether reservations are necessary, which credit cards are accepted, the average price for an a la carte meal, and the price for all prix fixe meals offered.

The following abbreviations are used in the restaurant listings:

To indicate annual vacation closing:
    No annual closing   NAC

To indicate credit cards accepted:
    American Express   AE
    Diners Club   DC
    MasterCard   MC
    Visa   V

To indicate if drinks are included in the prices quoted:
    Boissons compris (drinks included) BC
    Boissons non-compris (drinks *not* included) BNC

At the end of the restaurant section listed by arrondissements is a "Quick Reference Guide." This guide lists restaurants in the Big Splurge category, those offering continuous food service, those open on Sunday, and those open for part or all of August. Finally, there is a glossary of menu terms, an alphabetical index of the restaurants listed, and a page for reader comments.

TIPS ON CHEAP EATS DINING

1. Eat and drink a block or two away from the main boulevards and tourist attractions. The range in price for even a cup of coffee can be considerable.

2. In smaller restaurants, arrive early for the best selection of seats and food.

3. Eat where you see a crowd of French people. If a restaurant is either empty or full of tourists, assume the locals know something you do not and move on.

4. *Always* read the menu posted outside before going in. This will prevent you from finding that you don't like anything on the menu after you have already been seated, and avoid any unpleasant surprises when the bill comes.

5. Stay within the limits of the kitchen's power and respect it. Don't expect gourmet fare from a corner café, and don't go to a fine restaurant and order only a salad.

6. The prix fixe menu will always be the best value if you like what's offered and don't want to skip a course.

7. In more sophisticated and expensive restaurants, the secret is to go for lunch and order from the prix fixe menu, which usually costs a fraction of what it would for dinner, if it is even offered for dinner.

8. Order the plat du jour. It is not only the best value for your dining franc, it generally represents the freshest seasonal food available.

9. Order the house wine (*vin de la maison* or *vin ordinaire*). Order *une carafe de l'eau ordinaire* (tap water) rather than a bottle of mineral water.

10. Have your morning café au lait and croissant standing at the bar at the corner café. It will cost almost twice as much served at a table, or if you have it at your hotel.

11. For a really inexpensive lunch, the street *marchés* (see page 22) are the perfect places to pick up the fixings for a *déjeuner sur l'herbe* (lunch under a tree in the park). Lunch can be anything from a sandwich on a crusty baguette or a wedge of *tarte a l'oignon*, to a piece of cheese, a ripe pear, and a bottle of young Beaujolais wine.

12. Restaurants change their hours of opening and closing and annual vacation times to adjust to the constantly changing patterns of

tourism and economics. Many that once closed for all of August may now close for only a few days or weeks. All the information given in *Cheap Eats in Paris* was accurate at press time, but just to make sure, call ahead, especially on a holiday and during the months of July and August.

13. You will never get lost if you buy a copy of the *Plan de Paris par Arrondissement*. Do not leave your hotel without it. Available at most news kiosks and bookstores, it contains a detailed map of each arrondissement, the Métro stop, plus a wealth of other useful information. It is pocket sized, and every Parisian has one; you should too, if you will be in Paris for more than 48 hours.

General Information About French Dining

CAFÉS, BISTROS, BRASSERIES, RESTAURANTS, TEAROOMS, AND WINE BARS

"Is this a café, a bistro, a brasserie, or a restaurant?" This is the question many foreigners ask because so much confusion exists about the definitions of these words. The following explanations should help clear up that confusion.

CAFÉS

The French don't go to priests, doctors, or psychiatrists to talk over their problems; they sit in a café over a cup of coffee or a glass of wine and talk to each other.

—Eric Sevareid
"Town Meeting of the World,"
CBS Television, March 1966

For any visitor to Paris, the café is a living stage and the perfect place to feel the heartbeat and pulse of the city. For most French, it would be easier to change their religion than their favorite café where they gather with friends at precisely the same time every day. Depending on the area, it can be a café pouring a wake-up Calvados to workers at 4 A.M., the lunch spot for local merchants, a lively afternoon rendezvous for students, or a meeting place to have one-with-the-boys on the way home from work. People who are lonely find company, foreigners find a place to write postcards and an unbeatable spot to take the pulse of the city, countesses rub elbows with cab drivers, and everyone finds *égalité*.

In a café you can eat, drink, and sleep it off afterwards, meet your lover, play pinball, hide from your boss, read, write, order takeout sandwiches, make telephone calls, use the toilet, pet the lazy dog sprawled across the entrance, or sit at a table for as long as you like, engaging in prime people-watching. If the café is also a *tabac* you can buy cigarettes, pipes, postcards, stamps, razor blades, cheap watches, lottery tickets, and *telecartes*, the wallet-size cards that take the place of coins in public phone booths. If the café has a PMU sign, you can place a bet on your favorite horse or political candidate. Talk about convenience! No wonder there are thousands of cafés in Paris, one on almost every corner of the city.

Cafés don't try to be trendy. The management has never consulted a decorator and it doesn't listen to talk about *nouvelle cuisine* or any other food fad of the moment. At peak hours, the hectic, noisy, smoky ambience is part of the charm. The lunch hour is usually the liveliest time, with service by acrobatic waiters who commit orders to memory, run with plates full of food, and never mix an order or spill a drop. The hearty *bonne maman* food is offered at prices that even struggling students can afford.

Parisians are masters of the art of café sitting. Almost any time of the year, the most popular café tables are those on the sidewalk. These offer a window on contemporary life in Paris and allow you to linger for hours over one drink and perfect the Parisian art of doing nothing while watching the world pass by. In any café, it will cost less to stand at the bar than to have the same order served to you at a table. On the other hand, when you do sit at a table, you acquire privileges bordering on squatter's rights. If the table has a cloth or paper place mat, that means the table is only for patrons who want to eat. If it is bare, you are welcome to sit, have a drink, and stay as long as you like. No one will rush you or ask you to pay until you are ready to leave or the café is about to close.

BISTROS

Bistros make up the heart and soul of Paris dining, and their popularity continues to grow as the French return to the nostalgic cooking rooted in their past. The average French person eats out at least three or four times a week, usually at a bistro. Some are small, unpretentious family-run places with a handwritten menu and a decor that hasn't changed for 30 years. Others are quite elegant by comparison, with starched linens and formally clad waiters. In any bistro, the atmosphere is congenial, and the room is packed with loyalists who know every dish on the menu and who appreciate the fair prices. When you are hungry enough to dig into a steaming platter of rib-sticking fare, head for a bistro. Farm-kitchen renditions of pot-au-feu, *boeuf bourguignon*, Lyon sausages, thick *cassoulets*, duck *confit*, salt cod, and the quintessential bistro dessert, *tarte Tatin*, are the lost and found dishes that salute the robust cooking of the French countryside.

BRASSERIES

Brasserie is the French word for "brewery" and that means a connection with beer. Open from early morning until past midnight, brasseries are big, brightly lit, and perpetually packed with a noisy, high-energy crowd enjoying service in the best long-aproned tradition. At almost any time of day, you can delve into platters of *choucroute*, fresh shellfish, steaks, and chicory salads loaded with bacon and topped with a poached egg. Everything is washed down with bottles of Alsatian wine and cold beer. While reservations are appreciated, you can usually get a table without one.

RESTAURANTS

With more than 20,000 places to eat in Paris, any dining mood or whim can be met. A restaurant serves *only* full meals, at set times. They offer a complete menu and long wine lists; they are more formal in service, food preparation, and presentation than cafés, bistros, and brasseries. Because eating is such a serious business in France, most restaurants have only one seating, to allow for leisurely dining. No waiter worth his white apron would ever rush a French person through a meal in order to free the table for other diners. You can count on spending almost two hours for a serious lunch and at least three for a nice dinner. Do as the French do: relax, take your time with your meal, enjoy the wine, and be happy you are in Paris.

TEAROOMS (*SALONS DE THÉ*)

French tearooms are romantic and welcoming places for those looking for a relaxing lunch, a high-calorie shopping or sightseeing break, or an afternoon of quiet, unhurried conversation with an old friend. Almost every neighborhood has its *salon de thé*, and they are as different as their owners: some are elegant, some are quaint, and others are high-tech modern. They are hospitable places where you are always encouraged to get comfortable and stay a while. Tearooms often have a no-smoking policy, a friendly cat to pet, and an air of intellectualism.

WINE BARS

Bars à vin are all the rage in the City of Light. The friendly "in" rendezvous for Parisian pacesetters, wine bars also are a smart solution for visitors looking for a light meal from noon until late in the evening. Ranging from rustic to futuristic, they serve fine wines as well as little-known vintages by the glass or bottle, along with simple, light meals of salads, cold cuts, cheeses, and hot main dishes.

THE FRENCH MENU

Let's face it, whether it is neatly printed on an oversized menu in a fine restaurant, whitewashed on a bistro window, written in fading chalk on a blackboard in a brasserie, or handwritten on a purple-mimeographed sheet pinned to a café curtain, the French menu can be intimidating. This section was written to make eating in Paris less threatening. All French eating establishments must, by law, post a menu outside showing the prices of the food they serve. *Cheap Eats in Paris* gives you enough information about each restaurant listed so that you will know generally what to expect once you get there. When you arrive at a restaurant, read the posted menu *before* going in. This avoids unpleasant surprises and embarrassment in the event what is offered on that particular day doesn't appeal to your taste or budget.

When reading a menu, look at the *menu prix fixe* (sometimes called a *menu conseille*) as well as the a la carte menu. The prix fixe menu will usually consist of three courses: the *entrée* (first course), the *plat* (main course), and cheese and/or dessert—all for one price. The drinks (wine, beer, or mineral water) may or may not be included in the price. The prix fixe menu is often a terrific bargain, especially in higher-priced restaurants, where it enables those on a tighter budget to dine in luxury at a more reasonable price. The choices may be limited, but the value is always there. Be careful, however, because more and more higher-priced restaurants are offering the prix fixe menu for lunch *only*. If you opt for the prix fixe menu you will be expected to take all of the courses offered. If you only want one or two, and three are offered, there will be no reduction in price. Don't think that a three- or even a four-course meal will be too much to eat. A good French meal is balanced, and the portions are not large. Enjoy your meal the way the French do—slowly—and you won't feel over-fed.

Most restaurants also offer a la carte choices, and for those with lighter appetites, this often makes good sense because you are not paying for courses you don't want. On the a la carte menu, each course is priced separately. A word of caution: Always look very carefully at the prices of the a la carte choices, because the sum of the parts may add up to a very expensive meal compared to the prix fixe meal. Generally, if you triple the cost of the a la carte main course, you will get a figure close to the total bill for a three-course meal, including wine.

Once inside and seated, don't ask for the menu, ask for *a la carte*. That way you will get the complete listing of all the foods served, from appetizers to desserts, on *both* the prix fixe and a la carte menus. If you ask for "the menu," you will probably get a strange look from the waiter, cause some confusion, and possibly end up with the prix fixe meal, which is referred to as *le menu.*

When ordering, keep in mind what is likely to be fresh and in season, and consider, too, the specialties of the chef. The chef's specialities are sometimes starred or underlined in red on the menu. The day of the week is also important. Fish is always best on Fridays and worst on Mondays, when all the wholesale food markets in Paris are closed. Also, keep in mind where you are. If you are in a corner café complete with pinball machines and a *tabac* in the corner, don't expect the chef to perform magic with wild game or to dazzle you with high-rising soufflés.

In any restaurant one of the best choices for the main course is the *plat du jour* (the daily special). It changes every day, the ingredients are fresh and seasonal, and there is a rapid turnover because the dish has proven to be a winner with the regulars. It won't be a dish whose ingredients have been languishing in the refrigerator for several days or were relegated to the freezer due to lack of interest.

FOOD

There is no food in Paris, only cuisine.

— Anonymous

The French take dining very seriously. In most French restaurants, no matter how big or small, time is not of the essence. A meal is to be savored and enjoyed, not dispatched on the way to something else. This especially applies to dinner, which is often an event lasting the entire evening.

There was a time when one could honestly say, "You can't get a bad meal in Paris." With the influx of golden arches, pizza parlors, ethnic restaurants, and takeout and fast food, it is definitely possible to suffer at the hands of Paris dining. Despite all of this, there are few cities in the world where you can consistently eat as well as you can in Paris, and, if you plan carefully, you can have the gastronomic experience of a lifetime here for much less than you would spend in any other major city in the world.

Just as Paris fashions change, so do the demands of restaurant patrons. Not too long ago, dining before 8 P.M. was almost unheard of. Now, more and more restaurants are opening at 7 or 7:30 P.M. for dinner and staying open much later on Friday and Saturday nights. Many, too, are staying open during part of August, which a few years ago was absolutely unthinkable. Unfortunately, many of the long-standing restaurant standards regarding the waiter's dress have been dramatically relaxed. Levis, T-shirts, and tennis shoes have replaced black pants, bow ties, and long white aprons, especially in the cheaper places.

In response to the desire for lighter meals, wine bars and tearooms continue to be growth industries. Formula restaurants emphasizing either a limited two-course menu and rapid service, or offering a three-course meal with several selections for each course and wine, but no a la carte, are booming. In order to keep the cost of the food down and still cope with rising inflation, more and more restaurants are adopting the use of paper napkins and paper table coverings, the corners of which are then used by the waiter to tally the bill. The Parisian love affair with anything American, especially food, shows no signs of diminishing. Carrot cake, banana and zucchini muffins, brunch, chocolate chip cookies, cheese cake, brownies, Tex-Mex food, chili, baby back ribs, and pizza delivered to the door continue to win daily converts.

No matter what the recipe or the time of the year, a good French chef insists on the freshest ingredients, ignores frozen foods and substitutes, and doesn't cut corners or use artificial flavorings or preservatives. French eating establishments, from the humble mom and pop cafés to the great temples of gastronomy, seldom have teenagers working part time in the kitchen or waiting tables between classes. From the chef on down, the employees are dedicated personnel, and this makes a difference in everything from the quality of food on your plate to the service at your table.

BREAKFAST (*PETIT DÉJEUNER*)

Breakfast is served from 7 to 10 A.M. in most cafés.

Parisians do not have a good grasp of what constitutes a real American breakfast, so do yourself a favor and follow the French example: start the day at the corner café with a café au lait, a *grande crème* or a *chocolat chaud*, and a flaky croissant. If you insist on bacon and eggs or other staples of the American breakfast table, be prepared to pay dearly for them. Smart Cheap Eaters save their omelettes or ham and eggs for lunch.

LUNCH (*DÉJEUNER*)

The midday meal is served from noon to 2:30 P.M., with the last order taken about 30 minutes before closing.

If you face a deadline, or you do not want a full-blown meal at lunch, go to a café, a wine bar, a tearoom, a brasserie, or put together *le snack*. Do not try to rush through a meal at a restaurant, and please do not go into a restaurant and order just a salad or an appetizer. It just is not done, and you could be refused service. You will not be regarded well by the staff, and the result will be great embarrassment.

A surprising number of French eat their main meal at noon. Recognizing this, many places offer very good value prix fixe menus at lunch *only*. If you are on a real shoestring budget, or you like eating your main meal at noon, there are bargains in all categories of eateries. Many places have their biggest crowds at lunch, so if you don't have a reservation, keep this in mind and try to arrive ahead of the crunch to be assured a good seat.

Paris has many delightful parks—the Luxembourg Gardens, the Tuileries, Champ-de-Mars, Jardin des Plantes, and the Bois de Boulogne—not to mention the romantic banks of the Seine and the many pretty squares throughout the city. The street *marchés* and shopping streets are the perfect places to shop for a satisfying and inexpensive al fresco *pique-nique* lunch. (see "Marchés," page 22). Have your picnic on a warm day in one of Paris's lovely parks, and you will probably share your park bench with a French person on his or her lunch hour having a *pique-nique* too.

DINNER (*DÎNER*)

The evening meal is served from 7 or 7:30 to 10 or 10:30 P.M., with the last order being taken about 30 minutes before closing.

Dinner is a leisurely affair, with the lunchtime frenzy replaced by a quiet, more sedate mood. Eight o'clock or 8:30 is still the most popular dinner time. Few cafés serve dinner, so your best bet is a brasserie, a bistro, or a restaurant. If you want a light meal or a rather late one, go to a wine bar.

LE SNACK/FAST FOOD À LA FRANÇAISE

Not everyone wants to devote a large segment of the day to a long lunch. This is where *le snack* and fast food come in.

Fast food *à la française* means a crêpe from the corner stand, a sandwich to go (*pour emporter*) from a café or sandwich shop, a quiche or small pizza heated at the *boulangerie*, or something from the *charcuterie* or nearby *traiteur*. *Charcuteries* and *traiteurs* specialize in prepared salads, pâtés, *terrines*, whole roasted chickens, a variety of cooked dishes, and usually one or two daily specials. All items are packed to go, and sometimes you can get a plastic fork or spoon. Most grocery stores sell individual slices of cold meat and portions of cheese. Add a fresh baguette, yogurt, a piece or two of fruit, and a cold drink or a bottle of *vin ordinaire*, and you will have a cheap and filling meal for little outlay of time and money. You can also assemble your fast-food feast from the stalls of one of the colorful street *marchés* (see "Marchés," page 22) or shopping streets. The sky is the limit here for tempting gourmet meals on the run.

BOURGEOISE CUISINE

Nostalgia is "in" and *nouvelle cuisine* is "out," declare the culinary pundits in Paris. There's no doubt about it, bourgeoisie cuisine *à la grand'mère* continues to enjoy tremendous popularity in Paris. This reassuring, back-burner bistro fare is the traditional cooking on which the French have subsisted for years. On thousands of menus, you can expect to see its mainstays: duck, rabbit, *cassoulet*, pot-au-feu, *boeuf bourguignon*, *blanquette de veau*, *tarte Tatin*, and crème caramel.

NOUVELLE CUISINE

This term was coined by food critics Henry Gault and Christian Millau in the 1970s and is probably one of the most widely talked-about developments in French cooking in the past 50 years. *Nouvelle cuisine* scorns the use of rich and heavy sauces. It emphasizes instead a lighter style of classic French cooking with a greater use of vegetables, an imaginative combination of ingredients, and a stylish and colorful presentation of small servings—all undercooked just a little. Over time, most people have decided that many of the dishes were contrived and resulted in dining adventures they did not enjoy. As a result, the popularity of *nouvelle cuisine* is definitely on the decline.

REGIONAL CUISINE

Solid regional cooking from the provinces, once snubbed by food-lovers as parochial and unsophisticated, has made a remarkable comeback as the French dig closer to their roots to bring back favorites of the past. In Paris you can travel gastronomically throughout France and never leave the city limits. The finest regional cooking is to be found in the capital, and represents some of the best food you will ever eat.

The big brasseries feature German-influenced Alsatian specialties of steaming platters of sauerkraut, sausages, and bacon, German Riesling wines, and mugs of frosty beer. If a restaurant features food from the Savoy region next to the Swiss-Alpine border, look for a bounty of cheeses, fondues, and *raclettes*. Food from the southwest Basque area is spicy, influenced by its Spanish neighbor. Superb seafood comes from Brittany in the north and from Nice in the south. Food from Provence is heavy with herbs, garlic, olive oil, and tomatoes. You can sample bouillabaisse, *pistou*—a pungent paste of fresh basil, cheese, garlic, and olive oil—*salade niçoise*, and ratatouille made from eggplant, zucchini, garlic, sweet peppers, and tomatoes. Veal and lamb are gifts from Normandy, and hearty *cassoulets* and huge helpings signify the robust Auvergne cooking.

MEAT

The French eat their meat cooked much less than we do. Pink chicken is the norm, and "blue" beef (raw to most Americans) is considered the height of good eating. *Saignant* (rare) is only slightly better done, but *à point* (medium rare) approaches the edible. *Bien cuit* (well done) may still be dripping blood, but it is at least hot and most of it will be cooked. Some meats simply do not taste good when they are well cooked, and the waiter will tell you, "It can't be done." Trust him and order something else.

CHEESE

> The French will only be united under the threat of danger. No one can simply bring together a country that has over 265 kinds of cheese.
>
> — Charles de Gaulle

Actually, France produces more than 400 varieties of cheese, and the average French person consumes between 40 and 50 pounds of cheese per year. When dining in France, you will quickly recognize that cheese is a vital ingredient in any meal. Cheese is served after the main course, never as an appetizer, as in the United States. When you are presented the cheese tray, don't be afraid to branch out and select a variety you have never tasted. Who knows, you may become a convert. Don't worry if you see some mold around the edges, either. If a cheese doesn't mold a little, it is too pasteurized to be worth anything.

UNUSUAL FOODS

There's nothing discreet about French food. Remnants that are discarded in the United States are here transformed into gastronomical delicacies. You will encounter *rognons* (kidneys), *cervelles* (brains), *ris de veau* (sweetbreads), *mouton* (mutton), *andouilles and andouillettes* (chitterling sausages), *langue de boeuf* (beef tongue), and more. There are butchers selling only horse meat (you can recognize them by the golden horse head hanging over their shops), and those who make a living selling the ears, heads, feet, and tails of pigs. Depending on the season, you may also find *pintade* (guinea fowl), *sanglier* (wild boar), *chevreuil* (deer), and *civet de lièvre* (wild hare stew). Blood is often used to thicken sauces, especially in *civet de lièvre.* All of these dishes can be delicious, and the French excel in their preparation. They represent dining experiences you must try—at least once.

VEGETARIAN RESTAURANTS

A vegetarian in Paris can eat and drink very well. Gone are the days when one had to settle for boring meals of brown rice, overcooked vegetables, or a plate of *crudités* at the corner café, served with a cup of lukewarm tea. While vegetarianism in France is nowhere near what it is in the United States, it is gaining ground in Paris. Those who eat some cheese and fish will have the easiest time, but there are also havens for those who eat no animal or dairy products. There are several strictly macrobiotic restaurants, but most serve a wider range of dishes that are guaranteed to please every dedicated veggie lover as well as their carnivorous friends eager to jump on the bandwagon, if only for one or two meals.

MARCHÉS

The French shop for the meal, not for the week, and they measure the freshness of their food in minutes, not days. If you ask the fruit merchant if the pears are ripe, he will ask you at what time that day you will consume them, and then select just the right ones. Even though indoor *supermarchés* are all over Paris, every neighborhood *quartier* has its own *rue commerçante* (shopping street) or *marché volant* (roving market). These *marchés* offer an endless source of interest and insight into the hearts and minds of ordinary Parisians, and visiting one of them is a cultural experience you should not miss. Go in the late morning, gather the ingredients for a picnic lunch or supper, and admire the rows of produce arranged with the same care and precision you see in fine jewelry stores. Take your camera and a string bag, don't mind the crowds, watch your wallet, and enjoy these lively alternatives to the galleries, monuments, churches, and other must-see classic stops on every visitor's list. When dining out, order the food you have seen in the market. You can bet the chef has been there long before you to select perfectly ripe strawberries, fat spears of asparagus, the freshest fish, and the ripest cheeses that appear on the menu that day.

Rues commerçants

These permanent food-and-shopping streets are usually open from 9 A.M. to 1 P.M. and 4 to 7:30 P.M. Tuesday through Sunday.

Rue Montorgueil, 2nd, Métro Sentier or Étienne Marcel
Rue Mouffetard, 5th, Métro Monge
Rue de Buci, 6th, Métro Odéon

Rue Cler, 7th, Métro École-Militaire
Rue de Levis, 17th, Métro Villiers
Rue Poncelet, 17th, Métro Ternes
Rue Lepic, 18th, Métro Abbesses

Marchés couverts
Huge indoor markets that are open from 8 A.M. to 1 P.M. and 4 to
7:30 P.M., Tuesday through Saturday.
Marché Chateau d'Eau, 10th, rue du Château d'Eau and rue Bou-
chardon, Métro: Château d'Eau
Marché de Passy, 16th, corner of rue Bois-le-Vent and rue Duban,
Métro: La Muette

Marchés volants
Roving markets that move from neighborhood to neighborhood on
specific days. Open from 7 A.M. to 1 P.M. *only* on the days listed.
Monge, place Monge, 5th, Métro: Monge, Wednesday, Friday,
Sunday
Raspail, blvd. Raspail between rue du Cherche-Midi and rue de
Rennes, 6th, Métro: Rennes or Sèvres-Babylone, Tuesday, Friday,
Sunday (organic products)
Dupleix, blvd. de Grenelle between rue Lourmal and rue du Com-
merce, 15th, Métro: Dupleix or La Motte-Picquet-Grenelle, Wednesday,
Sunday
Cours de la Reine, avenue Président Wilson between rue Debrousse
and place Iéna, 16th, Métro: Alma-Marceau or Iéna, Wednesday,
Saturday

DRINKS

APERITIFS AND BETWEEN-MEAL DRINKS

The French prefer not to anesthetize their taste buds with American-
style cocktails before a meal. Instead of your usual dry Martini or a double
Scotch on the rocks, try one of the mildly alcoholic wine apéritifs such as a
kir or a *kir royale*. A *kir* is made from *crème de cassis* and chilled white wine.
A *kir royale* substitutes champagne for the wine. The slightly bitter Cam-
pari and soda is also a good choice.

If you are hot and thirsty in the afternoon, try a *Vittel menthe*: a shot
of crème de menthe diluted with Vittel mineral water and served icy cold.
It is one of the cheapest and most refreshing between-meal drinks. For a
nonalcoholic beverage, a good choice is *l'orange pressée* (fresh orange juice)

or *le citron pressé* (lemonade). Coca Cola (*Coka*) and Orangina, a carbonated orange drink, are popular soft drinks, but Perrier with a twist of lemon or lime is the favorite drink between meals.

France is not known for beer, but if you want a beer, don't say so. There is a French product, *Byrrh,* which sounds the same but it is a bitter quinine-based wine aperitif, and this is what you are likely to get if you order a "beer." If you want a draft beer, ask for *un demi* or *une bière à la pression.* Remember, it is pronounced "beair," not "beer." If you just ask for *une bière,* you will be asked what kind, because you will have ordered a bottle of beer. By the way, the best bottled beer in France is Kronenbourg.

COFFEE

The French consider it barbaric to drink coffee *with* a meal. Coffee is drunk after a meal, or by itself in a café, but *never, never* with the meal. It *may* be drunk with dessert, but you will receive an arched eyebrow from the waiter. French coffee is wonderful. It comes in various bewildering forms, all of which are stronger and more flavorful than American coffee. All coffee is served by the cup, and there are no free refills.

Café express, or *café noir,* is espresso coffee made by forcing hot steam through freshly ground coffee. If you prefer it weaker, ask for *café allongé* and you will be given a small pitcher of hot water to thin it.

Café crème is espresso with steamed milk, and café au lait is espresso with warmed milk. Neither of these is ordered after lunch or dinner. They are strictly breakfast or between-meal *boissons.*

Café filtre is filtered coffee that is the closest to American taste, but it's often available only in more expensive restaurants.

Déca, or *café décaféiné,* is decaffeinated espresso coffee. It bears the same resemblance to the tasteless U.S. version as a Rolls-Royce does to a bicycle.

Double and *grand* are terms used to request a double-sized cup of any of the above.

TEA

Tea is considered a breakfast or between-meal beverage, not an after-meal drink. Outside of a fancy tearoom, the tea you will be served will usually be of the tea-bag variety, and the water often will be tepid. Herbal teas (*infusions*) are refreshing afternoon drinks. The most popular are *tilleul* (linden), *menthe* (mint), and *verveine* (verbena). Iced tea is almost unheard of.

WATER

You could almost die of thirst before getting a simple glass of water in Paris. You won't automatically be served ice water the minute you sit down. If you want water, you must ask for it. If you are a purist, order bottled water, which is very popular and available everywhere. You will, however, be just as well off and money ahead, by ordering tap water (*une carafe d'eau*). Favorite bottled mineral waters are Evian and Vittel, which are still (*plate*), and Badoit and Perrier, which are sparkling (*gazeuse*). Perrier is usually a between-meal drink because the French consider it too gaseous to be drunk with meals.

WINE

Ask any well-fed Frenchman and he will tell you that a meal without wine is like a kiss without the squeeze. It is beyond the scope of *Cheap Eats in Paris* to attempt a thorough discussion of French wines or to provide a formula for selecting the perfect wine for every meal. If you're interested in saving money, however, order the house wine—*vin de la maison*—which is almost always a choice of red, white, or rosé, or a bottle from the patron's own *cave: cuvée du patron*. Either will be perfectly adequate and quite reasonably priced. The wine *carte* can be a budget killer, as most bottled vintages tend to drive up the cost of the meal inordinately. Unless you are a true wine connoisseur, it seems foolish to spend twice as much on the wine as on the food. You can bet that the Frenchman sitting next to you won't be doing it. If you do decide to branch out and you find the wine *carte* perplexing, don't be afraid to ask questions, state your budget, or take advice.

FRENCH DINING MANNERS

CROWDING

Don't be put off by location, appearance, or decor. A better gauge for judging a restaurant is how crowded it is with local French, because, as everyone knows, a full house is always a good sign. Crowded restaurants are an accepted fact of dining life in Paris, with the distance between tables often only one thin person wide.

You can't fight this phenomenon, and besides, being comfortably wedged in along a banquette leads to some mighty interesting benchmates and conversations.

DOGGIE BAGS

The French have more dogs per capita than any other people on earth. Short of being given the vote, dogs have many rights in Paris, not the least of which is dining out with their owners. While you will seldom see anyone under 18 in a restaurant, you will always see well-behaved dogs, especially in cafés, sitting on the seat next to their owner, or quietly lying at his or her feet. You would think this enormous dog population would create a demand for doggie bags, at least for the stay-at-home canines. Wrong. Despite the number of courses in a typical French meal, portions are smaller than most Americans are used to. Half of France is on some kind of diet, and leaving food on your plate is acceptable. Asking for a doggie bag, whether for Fido or yourself, is not.

MIND YOUR MANNERS AND DRESS FOR SUCCESS

Good manners are international, and *la politesse* is central to all transactions in France. The French are also more formal than we are. They preface statements with *"Pardon, Monsieur," "s'il vous plaît, Madame,"* or *"Excusez-moi, Mademoiselle."* They will consider you to be rude if you don't do the same or if you omit the words *monsieur, madame,* or *mademoiselle* when you speak to them. If you want good service, a *"Bonjour, Monsieur,"* or *"Merci, Mademoiselle,"* along with lots of *s'il vous plaît*s and *merci beaucoup*s thrown in will go a long way toward making your dining experience better.

To get the waiter's attention, don't shout *"Garcon!"* Contrary to popular belief, those who work in restaurants, in any size or price category, do not respond at all well to being addressed as *"Garcon!"* For best results, always refer to the waiter as *Monsieur* and the waitress as *Mademoiselle*, regardless of age or marital status.

It is considered very rude to eat your *frites* (French fries), chicken, or any food for that matter, with your fingers. It is not uncommon to see diners peeling a pear or other piece of fruit with a knife and fork.

Dressing well is very important in France, and especially in Paris. While men do not always need to wear a coat and tie and women don't need to feel they must dress to the nines, a little conservative good judgment is in order. The French have limited tolerance for the concept of sacrificing fashion for comfort. In addition, short shorts, halter tops, T-shirts with insignias, and baseball caps in restaurants are frowned on; they will immediately brand you as a *gauche* tourist.

SMOKING

Obviously, there is no French surgeon general extolling the virtues of a smoke-free environment. During the busiest times in cafés and bistros, it is nearly impossible to escape from the Gauloise-induced haze. In the *Cheap Eats in Paris* listings where smoking is prohibited, or where there is a specific nonsmoking section, it has been boldly noted. Otherwise—*bonne chance.*

RESERVATIONS

To avoid disappointment, it is always better to arrive with reservations. While reservations are not necessary in a café, they are essential in restaurants and in popular bistros and brasseries. If you arrive without a reservation, you might be told that the restaurant is *complet* (full) even when the tables are empty. The reason is that those empty tables have been reserved and are being held.

If you have a reservation for 8:30 or 9:00 P.M., don't be late. French restaurants honor their reservation times and don't relegate patrons to the bar to wait for the present occupants to gulp down the last drop of espresso before relinquishing their table. Many places have only one seating for either lunch or dinner, so if you change your plans after reserving, you should always call to cancel so that your table can be rebooked.

CLOSURES

Very few Paris eating establishments are open every day of the year. Most close at least one day a week, and sometimes for either lunch or dinner on Saturday and all day Sunday. Many close for public holidays, as well as for one week at Christmas and Easter. Some smaller family-run operations close for the school holidays in the fall and winter. The French consider their annual holiday time to be a God-given right. Despite government pleading and tourist demands, many still have an annual closing (*fermeture annuelle*) for all or parts of July and August. Closures also vary with the mood of the owner and adjust to the changing patterns of tourism and inflation. It is impossible to guarantee that this year's policy will carry over to the next. To avoid arriving at a restaurant only to find it closed, always call ahead to check, especially on a holiday and in July and August.

PAYING THE BILL

After the mysteries of the French menu, no subject is more confusing to foreigners than French restaurant bills. Your bill will not automatically be brought to your table at the end of the meal—you must ask for it (*"L'addition, s'il vous plait"*).

CREDIT CARDS

The acceptance of plastic money is second nature today in Paris, and it's possible to pay for most meals with a credit card. Policies often change, however, so when reserving, it is wise to double-check which cards the restaurant accepts. The most popular cards are Visa, known as *Carte Bleu*, and MasterCard, known as *Eurocard.*

The following abbreviations are used in the restaurant listings to show which credit cards are accepted:

American Express	AE
Diners Club	DC
MasterCard	MC
Visa	V

PRICES

In most cases, the bottom line on your restaurant bill will depend on your choice of wine. All the prices quoted in *Cheap Eats in Paris* are for one person and show whether or not drinks are included. In determining price quotations, the cheapest food on the menu was avoided, including such French favorites as tripe and *andouillettes*, which do not appeal to most Americans. The prices that are quoted represent the median cost of an a la carte meal with a starter (*entrée*), main course (*plat*), and dessert. All prices are quoted in French francs. Even though every attempt has been made to ensure the accuracy of the information given, a certain margin of error in pricing exists due to fluctuating exchange rates, inflation, escalating food costs, and the whims of restaurant owners.

SERVICE CHARGE

By law, all restaurants in France must include a 12 to 15 percent service charge in the price of all food served. This will be stated on the menu by the words *service compris* or *prix nets*. No additional service charge may be added to your bill. Always check your bill carefully, and if your waiter adds a service charge, by all means protest.

TIPPING

Remember, the service charge *is* the tip. In France you are obliged to tip the butcher, the delivery boy, and the theater usher, but not the waiter, not even in fine restaurants like Jamin and Taillevent. Although you are not required to pay one *sou* more, if the waiter has performed some extraordinary service, or you were particularly pleased, then an additional tip may be in order. Depending on the size and type of establishment, anything from a few francs to 5 or 10 percent of the bill would be appreciated. Regulars in cafés usually leave the small change.

RESTAURANTS BY ARRONDISSEMENT

Paris is divided into 20 districts, or zones, known as *arrondissements.* Knowing which arrondissement is which is the key to understanding Paris and quickly finding your way around. Starting with the first arrondissement, which is the district around the Louvre, the numbering goes clockwise in a spiral. The postal code, or zip code, for Paris is 750, followed by the number of the arrondissement. If you see 75002, you will know it is the 2nd arrondissement. The arrondissement for every restaurant is noted with every address given in *Cheap Eats in Paris*: (5th) means the fifth arrondissement; (18th) means the eighteenth.

Each arrondissement retains its own special character, so that Paris is, when you get to know her, a city of 20 neighborhood villages. Each has its own mayor, central post office, police station, and town hall where marriages and deaths are recorded. It takes a few afternoons of what the French call *flânerie,* unhurried, aimless wandering, to truly appreciate some of the more intriguing neighborhoods. You should be prepared to be sidetracked, diverted, and happily lost.

If you are going to be in Paris for more than one or two days, your smartest and most valuable purchase will be a copy of the *Plan de Paris par Arrondissement.* Available at all new kiosks and at bookstores, it contains a detailed map of every arrondissement, with a complete street index, Métro and bus routes, tourist sites, and much more.

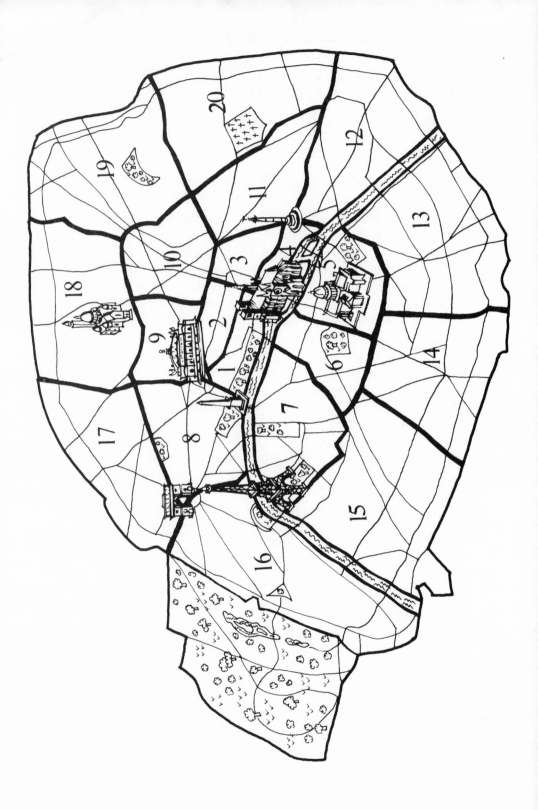

FIRST ARRONDISSEMENT

The Île de la Cité is the historic heart of Paris. It was on this island in the middle of the Seine that a Celtic tribe of fishermen called the Parisii settled in the third century B.C., and later that the Gallo-Romans built the city they called Lutetia in the first century A.D.

The history of Les Halles parallels the growth of Paris itself over the last 25 or 30 years. For decades Les Halles was the central wholesale food market in Paris. Nicknamed "the belly of Paris," it was an early-morning place of meat markets, fishmongers, fruit and vegetable sellers, and cheese merchants. In 1969, the market was moved to Rungis, on the outskirts of Paris, and in its place was built the Forum des Halles, a multilevel indoor shopping complex. The area around it now bursts with electricity and excitement. It positively teems night and day with an inexhaustible supply of people of every size, shape, and type who provide a real *tour de fashion.* While here you can watch a fire-eating act, listen to African bands, buy far-out fashions, get your hair colored or spiked, have safety pins put in your ear lobes, or see a triple-X-rated film.

Literally hundreds of restaurants are in this area, often opening and closing with the speed of rising and lowering hemlines. Some that have fallen on hard times in the past have been resurrected and given fast face lifts, but only a few serve worthwhile food, let alone charge reasonable prices. This is especially true along Rue St-Denis and the streets right around the Forum des Halles. If you are willing to walk five or ten minutes away from all this glitz, *Cheap Eats in Paris* will lead you to some of the best food you are likely to have on your entire visit.

FIRST ARRONDISSEMENT
Right Bank: Comédie Française, Conciergerie (where Marie Antoinette was beheaded), Île de la Cité, Pont Neuf (the oldest bridge in Paris), Les Halles, Louvre, Palais de Justice, Palais-Royal, Place Vendôme, Ste-Chapelle (with 1,500 square yards of blue and red stained glass)

FIRST ARRONDISSEMENT RESTAURANTS

À la Tour de Montlhéry
   (Chez Denise)

Au Chien Qui Fume
Batifol

Bistro d'Eustache
Chicago Meatpackers
Joe Allen
Juveniles
La Cordonnerie (Chez
   Yvette & Claude)
L'Ami Léon
La Potée des Halles
La Providence
Le Bèarn

L'Écluse
Le Cochon à l'Oreille
L'Emile
L'Épi d'Or
Lescure
Le Soufflé
Le Ver Luisant
L'Incroyable
Rose Thé

À la Tour de Montlhéry (Chez Denise)
5, rue des Prouvaires (1st)

TELEPHONE
42-36-21-82

MÉTRO
Les Halles, Louvre, Châtelet

OPEN
Mon–Fri 24 hours

CLOSED
Sat, Sun; July 14–Aug 15

HOURS
6 A.M. Mon–7 A.M. Sat,
nonstop

RESERVATIONS
Essential

CREDIT CARDS
MC, V

A LA CARTE
180–200F, BC

PRIX FIXE
None

"It's not good, it's wonderful!" That's what the man seated next to me told me the first time I ate here. After all, he should know; he has eaten here every day for years, and so have scores of other robust Frenchmen. If you are looking for a colorful and authentic Les Halles bistro that has not changed over the years, À la Tour de Montlhéry, or Chez Denise to the regulars, is a must. This classic spot is busy 24 hours a day with a colorful mixture of artists, *clochards*, businesspeople, and writers, served by surefooted white-aproned waiters who keep running and smiling despite the crunch. It is always jam-packed, the tables are small, and the noise level and blue haze of Gauloise smoke are typically French.

Eternity stands behind the chalkboard menu, and no dieters need apply: this is hearty food with portions that could be considered lethal by some. To start, order the snails in garlic butter or a simple salad of *frisée aux lardons*. Follow this with *tripes au Calvados,* leg of lamb, a tender rabbit in mustard sauce, or the wonderful stuffed cabbage. Complement your meal with a bottle of Brouilly, the house wine. The desserts should not be ignored, especially the plate of *profiteroles* swimming in warm chocolate sauce, or the *gâteau Marguerite,* laden with fresh strawberries and cream—both worth every extravagant bite.

Au Chien Qui Fume
33, rue du Pont-Neuf (1st)

The redeveloped Les Halles area of Paris has one of the strangest mixtures of cafés, bars, and restaurants in the city, patronized by an equally eclectic, often bizarre group of patrons. Since 1754 there has been a thriving restaurant on this site, serving everyone from Molière and his friends to the young and energized crowd that packs it today. The two-level restaurant with a garden terrace was completely restored to its original glory in the early eighties. In addition to very comfortable seating and proper service by waiters dressed in black vests and floor-length white aprons, Au Chien displays lots of brass, glass, fresh flowers, and an impressive collection of paintings of dogs. Because it is open daily from noon until way past midnight, this is a good place to remember if you are hungry at an odd hour. It is also a smart choice if you are with a group and everyone wants something different to eat. The menu is long and the well-prepared food is not at all fussy, but is as reliable as the regulars. The lineup of prix fixe possibilities, daily specials, fresh oysters and shellfish, beef, lamb, veal, and compelling desserts will please everyone, and so will the final tally on the bill.

TELEPHONE
42-36-07-42

MÉTRO
Châtelet

OPEN
Daily

CLOSED
Never; NAC

HOURS
Noon–2 A.M.

RESERVATIONS
Advised

CREDIT CARDS
AE, DC, MC, V

A LA CARTE
200F, BNC

PRIX FIXE
69F, 1 entrée and 1 plat or 1 plat and 1 dessert, BNC (noon–8 P.M.); 98F, 3 courses, BNC (noon–8 P.M.); 148F, aperitif, 3 courses, BNC (served anytime)

Batifol
14, rue Mondétour (1st)

Everyone knows that bistro dining in Paris is on the "in" list. True, Batifol is a chain and therefore not totally authentic, but these are lively and welcoming places with sensible prices that will appeal to all Cheap Eaters. For regulars and friends, a Batifol is the place to go when they don't want to dress up for an evening of casual food, good conversation, and pleasant ambience.

Although not especially innovative, the simple

TELEPHONE
42-36-85-50, 42-36-85-51

MÉTRO
Étienne-Marcel

OPEN
Daily

CLOSED
Never; NAC

HOURS
11 A.M.–1 A.M., continuous service

food is well prepared and the wine list short and cheap. Entrées include *chèvre chaud sur salade* (warm goat cheese on a bed of greens) and sliced tomatoes with fresh basil and mozzarella cheese. The specialties are *tête de veau ravigote* (head of veal in a vinaigrette sauce), pot-au-feu, and several grilled steaks with mixed herbs. For dessert, you won't regret saving room for the éclair filled with coffee or chocolate cream, or the Calvados-flavored *tarte Tatin*.

Bistro d'Eustache
37, rue Berger (1st)

RESERVATIONS
Advised for evening
CREDIT CARDS
AE, DC, MC, V
A LA CARTE
130F, BNC
PRIX FIXE
None

Patrons at Bistro d'Eustache are ageless, animated, and very casual. The Levis-clad staff are equally hip and having just as good a time as you are. When you arrive, take a seat at one of the wooden tables downstairs and fill yourself with the inexpensive bistro food. There are no gourmet surprises, just overflowing platters of the type of homey food that has been cooked in French kitchens for years: warm sausage with new potatoes, marinated herring, duck, leg of lamb with potato puree, crème caramel, chocolate mousse, fruit *tartes*—and the list goes on.

In the afternoons between 3 and 7 P.M., the first floor becomes something of a local neighborhood hangout and is a perfect place to doodle away an hour or so playing backgammon. Even if you don't play, it is nice to sit by a window overlooking St-Eustache, one of the loveliest churches in Paris.

TELEPHONE
40-26-23-20
MÉTRO
Les Halles
OPEN
Daily bar, lunch, and dinner
CLOSED
Major holidays; 15 days in January
HOURS
Bar Mon–Sat noon–4 A.M., Sun noon–2 A.M.; lunch noon–3 P.M., dinner 7–11 P.M.
RESERVATIONS
Advised on weekends
CREDIT CARDS
MC, V
A LA CARTE
115–125F, BNC
PRIX FIXE
None

Chicago Meatpackers
8, rue Coquillière (1st)

TELEPHONE
40-28-02-33
MÉTRO
Les Halles
OPEN
Daily
CLOSED
Never; NAC

The Midwestern twang of the Chicago WJMK radio disk jockey announces that it is 5:30 P.M. in Chicago and the commute is in its usual gridlock status, then introduces Frank Sinatra crooning "Chicago is my kinda town." If Chicago is your kind of town, then the Chicago Meatpackers in Les Halles is your kind of restaurant. Big, bright, and fast moving, it lets you know from the moment you enter that you are in for a good time.

The American food and drinks have rapidly won the hearts of Parisians who come to feast on baby back ribs, prime steaks, stuffed potato skins, onion loaf, garlic bread, five-way chili, chocolate chip cheesecake, and a rich mud pie to die for. At the huge mirror-lined bar, the friendly bartender mixes one of the driest Martinis in town, makes a lethal Singapore sling and a prize-winning bloody Mary, and pours Chicago Old Gold beer into ice-cold mugs. Children love the bibs, badges, and balloons; the magician who performs on Sunday mornings; the model Chicago & Pacific train running overhead; and the soda machine at the front that dispenses minibottles of all their favorites for only a dime.

Can't finish your Big Bopper hamburger or Meatpacker's barbecued chicken? Then ask for an official doggie bag, probably the only one you will see in Paris. The waiters and waitresses all speak English, the restaurant is open every day, and it is all a great taste of home. Don't miss it.

HOURS
11:30 A.M.–1 A.M., continuous service

RESERVATIONS
Not necessary

CREDIT CARDS
MC, V

A LA CARTE
110–120F

PRIX FIXE
Menu Express, lunch only: 80F (plat du jour, sandwich or half rack of ribs, dessert, and coffee)

Joe Allen
30, rue Pierre-Lescot (1st)

Joe Allen's New York–style saloon, with its brick walls, pine floors, and jukebox playing old favorites is one of the oldest and best American places in Paris. It is also one of the most popular gathering spots for the young French professionals, theater people, and late-nighters who pack Les Halles. Unless you want to stand at the bar and mingle with the crowd while waiting up to an hour for a table inside or on the summer terrace, dinner reservations are in order.

All American holidays are cause for celebration here. There is an honest-to-goodness Fourth of July party; for Halloween everyone dresses up in elaborate costumes; and the Thanksgiving celebration, where you can count on turkey and all the trimmings, is a Paris tradition. The chef always prepares a special

TELEPHONE
42-36-70-31

MÉTRO
Étienne-Marcel

OPEN
Daily

CLOSED
Never; NAC

HOURS
Noon–1 A.M., continuous service; bar closes 2 A.M.

RESERVATIONS
Dinner; American holidays

CREDIT CARDS
MC, V

A LA CARTE
150–170F

PRIX FIXE
None

menu for these occasions, and reservations are essential weeks in advance.

The American-style food is consistently good, and the menu is printed twice daily in English. If you are yearning for a great chili burger, a plate of tangy buffalo wings, a bowl of thick black bean soup, the best spinach salad in town, a piece of calorie-charged pecan pie made with imported Georgia pecans, a sinfully rich brownie, or a slab of banana cream pie, then go straight to Joe Allen's.

Juveniles
47, rue de Richelieu (1st)

TELEPHONE
42-97-46-49
MÉTRO
Palais-Royal
OPEN
Mon–Sat
CLOSED
Sun; NAC
HOURS
Noon–11 P.M, continuous service
RESERVATIONS
Not necessary
CREDIT CARDS
MC, V
A LA CARTE
50–110F
PRIX FIXE
Tapas for 2: 90F, BNC; 150F, BC

Serving food from noon until just before midnight, Juveniles is a smart address to remember if you want a light meal accompanied with a glass or two of a little–known Spanish or French wine.

Mark Williamson of Willy's Wine Bar fame and his partner Tim Johnson also operate this place, which specializes in less serious wines and Spanish *tapas*. The biggest part of the draw at Juveniles is the wine. Spanish and French country wines are poured, along with interesting varieties of Spanish sherry. In addition to a menu that includes salads, sandwiches served on bread from Jean-Luc Poujauran, and daily-changing hot dishes, Juveniles excels in *tapas*. These little plates can be ordered individually or as part of a prix fixe *tapas* menu. The assortment might include grilled sardines, chicken wings with a tangy tomato sauce, warm marinated beans topped with pieces of raw ham and red onions, and potato rounds covered with melted cheese or *anchoïade*, a spicy puree of anchovies, olive oil, and fresh garlic.

Chocolate-fanciers will want a slice of Donald's chocolate cake, and cheese-lovers will order a chunk of English Cheddar or Stilton blue cheese and a glass of ruby port to go with it.

La Cordonnerie (Chez Yvette & Claude)
20, rue St-Roch (1st)

Claude and his wife Yvette have been cooking and serving for 28 years in their little restaurant made up of two dining rooms and seating just 24 people. One room is dominated by the open kitchen with its enviable collection of copper cooking pots, pans, and molds; the other by a tiny bar, an antique icebox, and five red-cloth-covered tables with fresh flowers and crisp linen napkins. There is nothing chi-chi or *nouvelle* here, but the welcome is warm and the food is prepared with professional dedication and great care.

Claude, who is passionate about his cooking, knows how to dish up tantalizing renditions of soothing old-fashioned French food. He prepares everything here, including the ice creams and *sorbets*. I like to start my meal with a plate of well-dressed seasonal *crudités*, a half avocado with shrimp, or, in the summertime, a fragrant melon laced with port wine. Follow this with the plat du jour: an *escalope normande* or grilled lamb. During the fall, a dessert *must* is the *délice aux noix*, a macaroon-based cake covered with custard cream and nuts from the trees in Claude's own garden, then topped with another macaroon layer and whipped cream. Sound rich? It *is*, and it is absolutely delicious.

TELEPHONE
42-60-17-42

MÉTRO
Pyramides

OPEN
Mon–Fri lunch

CLOSED
Dinner; Sat, Sun; August; 2 weeks at Christmas; Easter; all holidays

HOURS
Lunch noon–2 P.M.

RESERVATIONS
Advised

CREDIT CARDS
None

A LA CARTE
150–160F, BC

PRIX FIXE
None

L'Ami Léon
11, rue Jean-Jacques Rousseau (1st)

What is that magic quality that makes discriminating diners zero in on a little place? Whatever it is, L'Ami Léon has it.

In my opinion, this restaurant is the perfect setting for the kind of meal one hopes to find in Paris. The interior reminds me of a country restaurant somewhere in the south of France. The nicely laid tables, with their own lamps and tiny bouquets of flowers, are placed far enough apart to ensure a peacefully intimate evening.

Everything is good here, from the bowl of nuts

TELEPHONE
42-33-06-20

MÉTRO
Louvre

OPEN
Mon–Fri lunch and dinner

CLOSED
Sat, Sun; holidays; Aug

HOURS
Lunch noon–2 P.M., dinner 8–9 P.M.

RESERVATIONS
Yes

CREDIT CARDS
MC, V
A LA CARTE
160F, BNC
PRIX FIXE
85F, 3 courses, BNC

placed on the table while you peruse the menu to the last drop of the *café express* and the chocolate that accompanies it. The menu is a bit limited, but nonetheless studded with treasures, all made by owner-chef Jean-Marie Léon Martin. The restaurant's many regulars are as enthusiastic as ever about the velvety chicken liver *terrine* appetizer. Main courses designed to please all meat and potato fans include choices of double lamb chops, *confit de canard,* and steak in a paprika and tarragon sauce. All are garnished with seasonally fresh vegetables and roasted potatoes. The desserts are overwhelmingly tempting, especially the flaky rhubarb and strawberry *tarte.*

La Potée des Halles
3, rue Etienne-Marcel (1st)

TELEPHONE
42-36-18-68
MÉTRO
Étienne-Marcel
OPEN
Mon–Fri lunch and dinner;
Sat dinner only
CLOSED
Sat lunch, Sun; Aug
HOURS
Lunch noon–2:30 P.M.,
dinner 7–10:30 P.M.
RESERVATIONS
Advised
CREDIT CARDS
AE, DC, MC, V
A LA CARTE
150–170F, BNC
PRIX FIXE
98F, 3 courses, BNC

Book ahead—you won't be the only one eager to eat in this haven of Paris nostalgia, which began as a café in 1906. Classified by the French government as a national historical monument, the restaurant, with its ornately hand-painted tiled walls portraying the goddesses of beer and coffee, still has its original chairs with brass plaques bearing the names of Les Halles workers who ate here every day when the wholesale food market of Paris dominated the area. Even today, some of these chairs are occupied daily by their 70- and 80-year-old "owners."

Unless you are ravenous, order a light *entrée* before your *plat* and plan to skip dessert. Instead, pay serious attention to the Auvergne specialty of the house, *la potée.* It comes in a big pot with white beans, cabbage, carrots, salt pork, ribs, smoked sausage, garlic butter, and cream. Other dishes high on the list include *ragoût de lotte au Sancerre,* a mild white fish stew, and for less robust appetites, the *aiguillette de canard au miel et citron*: thin slices of duck breast with a honey and lemon glaze. At the end of this *grand bouffe,* you will probably stagger away a little heavier, but definitely well satisfied.

La Providence
6, rue de la Sourdière, corner of 308 rue St-Honoré (1st)

La Providence, once a neighborhood secret, is now out in the open. This authentic bistro with its multi-colored tile floors, beamed ceiling with slow-moving fans, paper-covered tables, and Art Deco lighting, has hardly changed from the days it served as the dining room of a *pension* for blue-collar workers.

Today it is perpetually crowded with savvy Parisians enjoying the robust fare inspired by owner Pierre Schweitzer's native Alsace-Lorraine region of eastern France. There is no need to consider straying from the three bargain prix fixe menus, which feature all the bistro standbys and many specialties as well. Alsatian wines are the call of the day here. If you are a real wine afficionado, ask M. Schweitzer for his recommendations. He stocks over 40 varieties, many of which are little known outside their native area.

On a cold winter night, request a table in the basement *weinstub*, a faithful re-creation complete with heart-shaped wooden chairs, provincial print fabrics, and old stone walls.

TELEPHONE
42-60-46-13

MÉTRO
Tuileries

OPEN
Mon–Fri lunch and dinner

CLOSED
Sat, Sun; holidays, NAC

HOURS
Lunch noon–2:30 P.M., dinner 7:30–11 P.M.

RESERVATIONS
Advised

CREDIT CARDS
AE, DC, MC, V

A LA CARTE
150F, BNC

PRIX FIXE
Lunch only: 78F, 2 courses, BNC, or 102F, 3 courses, BNC; dinner only: 109F, 2 courses plus cheese, or dessert, or coffee, or wine

Le Béarn
2, place Ste-Opportune (1st)

In addition to being a refreshingly cheap eat, Le Béarn is a great place to hone your people-watching skills. In the morning, you are likely to find workers with red-vein-webbed cheeks sitting at the bar, lingering over what is obviously not their first glass of *vin rouge* of the day. A predominantly young crowd, of every conceivable orientation and dress, pours in at lunch-time to take advantage of the low-priced plats du jour, which come in pre-*nouvelle*-sized portions. These are usually overflowing plates of no-nonsense meats, accompanied with equally serious potatoes. Unless it's raining or freezing cold, the outside tables on the Place Ste-Opportune are *the* places to sit. From these perches, you will have a front-row van-

TELEPHONE
42-36-93-35

MÉTRO
Châtelet

OPEN
Mon–Sat bar and lunch in winter, daily rest of year

CLOSED
Sun in winter; holidays; 5 days around Aug 15

HOURS
Bar 8 A.M–9 P.M., lunch noon–3:30 P.M.

RESERVATIONS
No

CREDIT CARDS
None

A LA CARTE
70F, BC
PRIX FIXE
None

tage point to watch the Les Halles fashion victims preen and prance around the *place* and the crowds surge out of the Métro stop just next to it.

L'Écluse (Les Halles)
rue Mondétour (1st)

TELEPHONE
40-41-08-73
MÉTRO
Étienne-Marcel
OPEN
Daily
CLOSED
Never; NAC
HOURS
Noon–1 A.M., continuous service
RESERVATIONS
No
CREDIT CARDS
MC, V
A LA CARTE
50–100F, BNC
PRIX FIXE
None

L'Écluse was a trailblazer in popularizing wine bars in Paris, and it is still one of the best. Offering wines by the glass or the bottle, these trendy spots cater to those seeking good wine and light, uncomplicated meals served in agreeable surroundings, with the final bill depending on the modesty or the majesty of the vintage chosen.

Specializing in Bordeaux wines, all five L'Écluse locations have the same menu, but each wine bar features a different type of Bordeaux wine. The upmarket clientele drops by from noon into the wee hours to sample wines ranging in price from 15F for a simple glass to over 250F for a bottle of a *grand cru.* The food is selected to go with the varieties of Bordeaux wine served, and everything is a la carte. Featured are house *terrines, rillettes, foie gras,* smoked salmon, daily hot and cold plates, and a famous diet-destroying chocolate cake.

Le Cochon à l'Oreille
15, rue Montmartre (1st)

TELEPHONE
42-36-07-56
MÉTRO
Châtelet
OPEN
Mon–Sat
CLOSED
Dinner; Sun; holidays; NAC
HOURS
4 A.M.–5 P.M., continuous service
RESERVATIONS
No
CREDIT CARDS
None
A LA CARTE
60–80F, BC
PRIX FIXE
None

The business hours of this tiny bar in Les Halles will give you some hint of its clientele, By 5:30 or 6 A.M., the place is alive with local workers and tradesmen with red faces and blue coveralls drinking their early-morning Cognac and coffee. Lunchtime is the same, when they flock in for the daily special and a bottle of red, or a hefty sandwich on a crispy baguette and a tall beer. If you don't want to get up at the crack of dawn or rub elbows with the locals at lunch, then do stop by for a coffee or a drink to admire one of the most beautiful small workingman's haunts still intact in Paris, with its original zinc bar and superbly detailed faïence mural depicting Les Halles market at the turn of the century.

L'Emile

76, rue Jean-Jacques Rousseau, corner of rue Etienne-Marcel (1st)

Peach linens set against forest-green banguettes, a beautifully carved bar, Art Nouveau lights, and an impressive collection of Erté number posters form the background for dining at L'Emile, a wonderful new find only a short walk from Les Halles, and yet a world away from the tourist trail.

The lively neighborhood crowd of diners, who, judging from all the hugging and kissing that goes on, know each other well, is matched by the warm and attentive welcome from proprietors Nicole Moreau and Benoit Isorni. An added classic note is Vicks, the bilingual dog, who nuzzles up to the patrons and supervises the door.

When dining at L'Emile, you can expect a seasonally changing menu of delicious pleasures. In the spring, it is nice to begin with the salad of tiny French green beans dressed in a raspberry vinaigrette, or the *oeufs en meurette*: poached eggs in red wine sauce with pieces of bacon and small onions. Their main-dish specialties, *fricassée de poulet au vinaigre de Xérès* (chicken in a sherry vinegar sauce) and *foie de veau au raisins* (liver with raisins) are generous, satisfying, and meltingly tender. Desserts such as the *fondant au chocolat noir* (chocolate cake with chocolate mousse) or *pain perdu à la cannelle* (similar to French toast with cinnamon) will leave you with sweet memories of a truly wonderful meal in Paris. Who could ask for anything more?

TELEPHONE
42-36-58-58

MÉTRO
Étienne-Marcel

OPEN
Mon–Fri lunch and dinner, Sat dinner only

CLOSED
Sat lunch, Sun; holidays; 1st week in May, 1 week between Christmas and New Year's; Aug

HOURS
Lunch noon–2 P.M., dinner 8–midnight

RESERVATIONS
Yes

CREDIT CARDS
V

A LA CARTE
190F, BNC

PRIX FIXE
Lunch only: 78F, 3 courses, BNC

L'Épi d'Or

25, rue Jean-Jacques Rousseau (1st)

L'Épi d'Or typifies what eating in Paris is all about: middle-aged waiters in black pants and long white aprons, serving traditional food in oversized portions to legions of habitúes of all ages who dine here regularly and until very, very late. The decor is cluttered, the place crowded, the seats hard, and the one toilet is an antique from Turkey, but the food and atmosphere are oh, *sooo* French.

TELEPHONE
42-36-38-12

MÉTRO
Louvre

OPEN
Mon–Fri lunch and dinner; Sat dinner only

CLOSED
Sat lunch, Sun; 1 week in winter

To enjoy the best flavor of L'Épi d'Or, reserve for an 8:30 dinner and be on time, or your reservation might be given away. The best value here is the set menu. Stick with the daily specials written on the blackboard or, depending on the season, order one of the filling servings of *jambonneau à la lyonnaise* (cured pork), *foie de veau* (veal liver), or the popular steak *tartare de l'Épi d'Or.* There is no reason to look beyond the very drinkable house red, white, or rosé wine. Finish the feast with a slice of *délice de l'Épi d'Or*, a double-chocolate walnut cake surrounded by a rich *crème anglaise*, or a piece of the *tarte Tatin au Calvados*, a 5-kilogram wonder that looks like a giant soufflé. If you are not up to one of these finales, at least sample a selection of the Berthillon ice cream or *sorbet*. A meal here is guaranteed to fill you to your toes, and you will leave happy and satisfied, probably swearing never to eat again.

Lescure
7, rue de Mondovi (1st)

Join the scores of readers, friends, and Parisians who continue to sing the praises of Lescure, one of the most popular restaurants listed in *Cheap Eats in Paris.* Located at the end of a short street just around the corner from Place de la Concorde, the restaurant was founded in 1919 by Leon Lescure. Today it is still owned and operated by the second generation of his family, who faithfully maintain his high standards of serving serious French bourgeoise cuisine at very reasonable prices. For both lunch and dinner, diners vie for one of the sidewalk tables, or sit elbow-to-elbow inside beneath ropes of garlic and country sausages dangling from the rafters. The service is friendly and is perhaps the fastest in Paris.

Look for the specials of the day written in red on the menu. One of the best and most available dishes is the *poularde au riz basquaise*: tender chicken served with rice and covered with a tangy tomato and green pepper sauce. Other favorites include the *confit de canard maison, boeuf bourguignon,* and the poached haddock. The most popular dessert is the special fruit *tarte* of the day.

Le Soufflé
36, rue de Mont-Thabor (1st)

Many savvy Parisians as well as informed visitors know that in this uncertain world, Le Soufflé is one restaurant you can always count on for a wonderful meal. After dining here, you will know you are in heaven—or at least in Paris. An interior glowing with soft lighting, pale pink walls, fresh flowers in miniature soufflé pots on each table, heavy cutlery, beautiful china, sparkling crystal, and service by polite and discreet waiters set the tone for Le Soufflé as it maintains its mandate on memorable dining in Paris. After all, what could be more Parisian than a soufflé? Whether you order a fluffy cheese, a delicate smoked salmon, a rich chocolate, or a Grand Marnier soufflé, or any of the other imaginative offerings, you will enjoy dramatic dining guaranteed to please even the most jaded palate.

In addition to the fantasia of soufflés, there are many appealing seasonal appetizers, hearty main courses, and luscious desserts. At the height of the spring season, the fat white asparagus vinaigrette is a definite must. The fresh artichokes dressed in a tangy lemon sauce is another popular *entrée*. For apple lovers, the *tarte fine aux pommes chaudes* is a dreamy dessert raising this standard on most French menus to new heights. Whatever you have at Le Soufflé will be divine and well worth the extra *centimes*.

TELEPHONE
42-60-27-19

MÉTRO
Concorde

OPEN
Mon–Sat lunch and dinner

CLOSED
Sun; holidays; NAC

HOURS
Lunch noon–2:30 P.M., dinner 7–10:30 P.M.

RESERVATIONS
Essential, several days in advance if possible

CREDIT CARDS
AE, DC, MC, V

A LA CARTE
160–200F, BNC

PRIX FIXE
190F, 4 courses, BNC

La Ver Luisant
26, rue du Mont-Thabor (1st)

Casual observers might think that this is just another ordinary café in central Paris and, seeing the lunch crowd, figure something is being given away. They are partially right. It *is* another café, and something *is* being (almost) given away: the food. Two important things, however, set this café apart from

TELEPHONE
42-60-83-69

MÉTRO
Concorde

OPEN
Mon–Sat bar and lunch

CLOSED
Dinner; Sun; holidays; Aug

HOURS
Bar 7 A.M., lunch noon–
2:30 P.M.

RESERVATIONS
No

CREDIT CARDS
None

A LA CARTE
70F, BNC

PRIX FIXE
59F, 3 courses, BNC

the rest in the *quartier*. First, it is clean, almost antiseptically clean, and second, the prices are impossible to beat in this top-drawer neighborhood that includes the Ritz and Crillon hotels, as well as the famed boutiques of Chanel, Yves St-Laurent, Ungaro, and many more.

Plain and simple café food is served to the silk-blouse and club-tie set, who sit at tables set with linen napkins (in a café, no less!), or at one of the two sidewalk seats. At all costs, insiders avoid the airless downstairs room next to the toilet and mop closet.

The menu includes all the standards: *crudités, rillettes, oeuf dur mayonnaise,* grilled sausage or steak with *frites,* the *plat du jour,* fruit *tartes,* chocolate mousse, and crème caramel. Nothing to remember from a gourmet's point of view, but from the point of view of a Cheap Eater hungry after a morning at the Louvre, this *is* a place to remember.

L'Incroyable
26, rue de Richelieu, and
23, rue de Montpensier (1st)

TELEPHONE
46-96-24-64

MÉTRO
Palais-Royal

OPEN
Tues–Fri lunch and dinner,
Mon and Sat, lunch only

CLOSED
Sat dinner, Mon dinner, Sun;
holidays; 15 days in July or Aug

HOURS
Lunch 11:45 A.M.–2:15 P.M.,
dinner 6:30–8:30 P.M.

RESERVATIONS
No

CREDIT CARDS
None

A LA CARTE
Dinner only: 90F, BNC

PRIX FIXE
Lunch: 55F, BNC; dinner:
65F, BNC

"The Incredible" is aptly named, with its three-course prix fixe menu going for less than $11 for lunch and $13 for dinner. It may not be as cheap as it used to be, and the quality can be spotty, but it is still a Cheap Eat worth considering. For this price, you can't expect smoked salmon or pheasant under glass served by waiters in tuxedos, but you can expect the usual basics of home-style *pâtés,* chicken, beef and pork, vegetables, simple salads, and unassuming desserts. Stick with the prix fixe menu and the daily specials and you probably won't be disappointed.

Getting to L'Incroyable is half the fun, because it is hidden in a narrow passage running between two streets near the Palais-Royal (thus the two addresses). When you're looking for this place, it is easy to imagine Paris as it must have been a century ago. Once you've found it, settle in either the flower-filled courtyard adjoining the two-room restaurant, or inside one of the cluttered dining rooms, and enjoy a good-natured inexpensive Paris meal.

Rose Thé
91, rue St-Honoré (1st)

Rose Thé can be found at the end of the Village St-Honoré, a narrow alleyway filled with dealers of antiques and bric-a-brac, just minutes away from all the noise and glitter of the Forum des Halles and Beaubourg. The inside of this napkin-sized tearoom is painted pastel pink and has a large Oriental rug covering most of the hardwood floor. Frilly white doilies on pink place mats and bouquets of fresh and dried flowers grace different styles of tables overlooking the plant-filled courtyard and the shops. Big armchairs and soft background music stress comfort and encourage long stays, making this a relaxing choice for a quiet lunch, a late-afternoon meal, or a peaceful teatime treat. Everything is made fresh daily in the tiny kitchen and is utterly delicious. Sample a bowl of the homemade soup, the savory *tarte du jour*, a perfectly tossed pasta salad bursting with flavorful herbs, or the satiny-rich rice pudding. For an afternoon delight, order the dense *fondant au chocolat* or the creamy cheesecake. On your way out, pay special attention to the shop on the corner of the Village St-Honoré that deals in magnificent antique silver.

TELEPHONE
42-36-97-18

MÉTRO
Louvre

OPEN
Mon–Sat lunch and tea

CLOSED
Sun; holidays; Aug

HOURS
Lunch noon–5 P.M.,
tea 2–6:30 P.M.

RESERVATIONS
Accepted, but not necessary

CREDIT CARDS
None

A LA CARTE
60–90F, BNC

PRIX FIXE
None

SECOND ARRONDISSEMENT

SECOND ARRONDISSEMENT
Right Bank: Bibliothèque
Nationale, Bourse, Cognacq-
Jay Museum, *passages*, Place des
Victoires

The second arrondissement is hardly a tourist hub in comparison to some others. It is the home of the stock market (Bourse). It is also dotted with *passages*: those relics of the-time-before-department-stores that were the shopping malls of the early 1900s. (See *Cheap Sleeps in Paris* for a listing of the most interesting passages.)

SECOND ARRONDISSEMENT RESTAURANTS

À la Perdrix	La Crémerie Louvois
Aux Caves de Bourgogne	L'Amanguier
Aux Lyonnais	La Patata
Chartier-Drouot	Le Vaudeville
Claude Brissemoret	Lina's Sandwiches
Country Life	Matinée-Soirée
Coup de Coeur	

À la Perdrix
6, rue Mandar (2nd)

TELEPHONE
42-36-83-21
MÉTRO
Sentier, Étienne-Marcel
OPEN
Mon–Fri lunch and dinner,
Sat lunch only
CLOSED
Sat dinner (except groups by
prior arrangement), Sun;
holidays; 1 week in Aug
HOURS
Lunch noon–3 P.M.,
dinner 6:30–10:30 P.M.
RESERVATIONS
For more than 4; Sat dinner
for large groups
CREDIT CARDS
MC, V
A LA CARTE
115–140F, BNC
PRIX FIXE
Lunch only: 55F, 3 courses,
BC; lunch and dinner: 79F and
98F, 3 courses, BNC

You can go with a slim wallet and a big appetite to À la Perdrix and find simple food served in a homey dining room that is scrubbed and polished every day. This long-standing Cheap Eat for neighbors and visitors alike is just off Rue Montorgueil, one of the most animated shopping streets in Paris.

The regulars don't have to consult the menu; they just wait for the waitress to tell them what is best that day. The three prix fixe menus are bargains and include favorites everyone knows and loves. Even the least expensive lunch menu, which changes daily, has a variety of choices for each course. Big spenders can opt for the most expensive menu and select between shrimp cocktail, a half-dozen snails, *crudités*, or a homemade *terrine* for the *entrée*, and salmon, *faux filet*, or stewed chicken for the main course. A piece of Camembert cheese or the dessert of the day ends the meal perfectly. All this is presided over by the friendly, cigar-smoking host, M. Benamou, who will encourage you to return. And when you do, you will be made to feel you are dining among family and friends.

Aux Caves de Bourgogne
3, rue Palestro (2nd)

Visitors to Paris often miss this spot, but it is a solid favorite with locals who come for the warm, friendly atmosphere and old-fashioned Bourgogne cooking served by the Seyot family. The reasonably priced, superb-quality lunch and dinner menu usually keep the place packed, so you are well advised to call ahead for reservations. When you call, ask to be seated along the back banquette, where you can best admire the beamed ceiling and impressive collection of farm equipment scattered around the room. If you like *boeuf bourguignon*, it is a *must* here. So is the *fondue bourguignonne*, with a choice of seven dipping sauces. More adventurous diners will want to sample the spicy *andouillette* (chitterling sausage) in Dijon mustard sauce or the steak *tartare*. All *plats* are served with a green salad or potatoes. The not-to-be-forgotten dessert is the caramelized *tarte Tatin*, served either flaming or with *crème fraîche*.

TELEPHONE
42-36-38-55

MÉTRO
Réaumur-Sebastapol

OPEN
Mon–Fri lunch and dinner; Sat dinner only

CLOSED
Sat lunch, Sun; holidays; June through Sept

HOURS
Lunch noon–2 P.M., dinner 7:30–10 P.M.

RESERVATIONS
Yes

CREDIT CARDS
MC, V

A LA CARTE
110F, BNC

PRIX FIXE
75F, 3 courses, BNC

Aux Lyonnais
32, rue St-Marc (2nd)

What more can anyone ask of a bistro? Pretty surroundings, interesting people, reliable food, honest prices—Aux Lyonnais has them all. At lunch it hums with the voices of office workers and stockbrokers from the Bourse and the matronly waitresses in black rushing to serve them. In the evening, the pace slows, and the service and mood become more relaxed and refined.

The menu offers dishes that have been served in bistros for generations. The first-rate fare is well prepared, with no unpleasant surprises. You will start with crispy baguettes spread with sweet butter. *Entrées*

TELEPHONE
42-96-65-04

MÉTRO
Bourse

OPEN
Mon–Fri lunch and dinner; Sat dinner only

CLOSED
Sat lunch, Sun; NAC

HOURS
Lunch 11:30 A.M.–3 P.M., dinner 6:30–10:30 P.M.

RESERVATIONS
Advised

CREDIT CARDS
AE, DC, MC, V

A LA CARTE
150F, BNC

PRIX FIXE
None

include a salad with warm sausage or chicken livers, a fish *terrine*, or a trio of spicy sausage patties covered in herbs and lightly sautéed. Salmon, creamed chicken with mushrooms, grilled lamb chops with spinach, and a tender rabbit covered in shallots, all served with *gratin dauphinois* (potatoes baked in cream), highlight the main dishes. The dessert not to miss is the floating island served in a large sundae dish and topped with a caramel glaze.

Chartier-Drouot/Chartier-Montmartre
103, rue de Richelieu (2nd)

TELEPHONE
42-96-68-23

MÉTRO
Richelieu-Drouot

OPEN
Daily lunch and dinner

CLOSED
Never; NAC

HOURS
Lunch 11:30 A.M.–3 P.M.,
dinner 6:30–10 P.M.

RESERVATIONS
No

CREDIT CARDS
None

A LA CARTE
60F–80F, BNC

PRIX FIXE
75F, 3 courses, BC

You can trust a Frenchman to know a good food bargain when he smells it. These two restaurants under the same management are major bargain destinations in the Cheap Eats game. Not much has changed over the years in these authentic Parisian soup kitchens with their fin de siècle decor, squads of brusque white-aproned waiters, and basic "no-parsley" food. There is no glamor or tinsel here. Big, noisy, barnlike, and jam-packed all the time, these are the blue-collar-worker's Maxim's, and workingmen and many others eat here in droves every day of the year.

The menu, which changes daily, is the same in both restaurants. Order only dishes that have to be made to order and save the fancier fare for another place. You could begin with a salad of tomatoes and cucumbers, or one of grated carrots with lemon. Order a jug of the house red or white wine to go with your main course of grilled salmon or lamb chops. All garnishes are extra, but only by a few francs. The most reliable dessert is an ice cream sundae or a piece of fresh fruit. If you choose carefully, you will have a satisfying and cheap meal.

Claude Brissemoret
5, rue St-Marc (2nd)

TELEPHONE
42-36-91-72

MÉTRO
Bourse

Claude Brissemoret is one of those special places you must know about beforehand. Once there, don't be put off by the drab interior, which has not changed for years. Fans of Claude Brissemoret who come here to enjoy his unpretentious bourgeoise cuisine, book this tiny 25-seat restaurant days ahead for both lunch and dinner. After one or two bites of his delicious food, the absence of decor won't really matter; you will be too busy concentrating on the meal in front of you to notice. Whatever you order will be seasonally fresh, cooked to perfection, and correctly presented. Good a la carte selections are the *rillons flambés au Cognac* (crisp pork belly sautéed in Cognac), the *fonds d'artichauds frais* (fresh artichoke hearts), and the *champignons frais à la crème* (fresh mushrooms in a cream sauce). Solid main dishes include the *fricassée de pintade aux fruits* (guinea hen with apricots, carrots, and lightly sautéed cabbage), and the *rognons de veau au curry* (curried veal kidneys). Save a little room for dessert and order the lightly poached pear in red wine, or the specialty: dark chocolate cake circled by a creamy custard sauce.

There is little more to say, except that this restaurant is a real treat, and—just remember—you can't eat the decor.

OPEN
Mon–Fri lunch and dinner

CLOSED
Sat, Sun; annual closing varies

HOURS
Lunch noon–2:15 P.M.,
dinner 8–11:30 P.M.

RESERVATIONS
Essential

CREDIT CARDS
MC, V

A LA CARTE
170F, BNC

PRIX FIXE
None

Country Life
6, rue Daunou (2nd)

The vegetarian tourist en route to Paris need not fear the only nourishment available will be omelettes, *frites*, and *crudités* at the corner café. Almost every practicing vegetarian in Paris knows about Country Life on the Rue Daunou, near the Opéra and across the street from Harry's New York Bar. Harry's advertisement "Tell the taxi driver 'sank, roo dough noo'" will also get you to Country Life.

As you enter, you walk through their natural products shop and natural foods bookstore. It is worthwhile to browse here if you are into herbal cosmetics, natural supplements, and herbal teas. In the back, the restaurant offers an expansive, all-you-can-eat, serve-yourself, hot-and-cold buffet and varied-salad bar. The daily-changing choices always include a

TELEPHONE
42-97-48-51

MÉTRO
Opéra

OPEN
Mon–Fri lunch only

CLOSED
Dinner; Sat, Sun; holidays;
NAC

HOURS
Restaurant Mon–Fri
11:30 A.M.–2:30 P.M.,
shop Mon-Thur 10 A.M.–
6:30 P.M., Fri 10 A.M.–3 P.M.

RESERVATIONS
No

CREDIT CARDS
AE, DC, MC, V

soup, several grain dishes, potatoes, assorted veggies, and desserts. Don't plan on ordering booze, coffee, or tea because they don't serve them. You can order fresh juice, mineral water, or a fruit shake to accompany your meal. There are two floors with plain pine tables, white tiles, and hanging green plants. No smoking.

Coup de Coeur
19, rue St-Augustin (2nd)

An eye-catching high-tech interior in soft shades of melon accented by Philippe Starck–designed dining chairs sets the mood for this sophisticated two-level restaurant catering to young, upscale patrons. Outgoing host Didier Oudin is at the helm, offering seasonally fresh cuisine that is intelligently prepared and beautifully presented. The only problem is not being able to select from all the creative offerings. For weight-watchers, the a la carte menu is starred with those dishes that are especially low in calories, and emphasizes several *entrée*, *plat*, and dessert combinations that add up to a total of less than 650 calories. In addition to the waist-slimming choices, there are two prix fixe menus. The best for my money is the 160F three-course selection that includes a choice of three aperitifs and a half bottle of wine. A good beginning for anyone ordering this is the *charlotte d'avocat au saumon fumé* (molded avocado with smoked salmon) or the *terrine des legumes, coulis des tomates* (a vegetable *terrine* with a fresh tomato sauce). Interesting *plats* are the *pintade grille aux pâtes fraîches* (grilled guinea hen with fresh pasta) and the *daurade au fou, crouquant d'endives* (baked sea beam with crispy endives). A conscience-calming dessert of mixed fresh fruits or a tangy *tarte citron* will round out this stylish meal.

La Crémerie Louvois
5, rue Louvois (2nd)

You don't have to be down and out in Paris to eat

here, but it is a great place to come if you are. It is also a useful Cheap Eat if you are bound for shopping around Place des Victoires or have just come from the Opéra.

The little room is ultra-casual, to say the least. There are only six tables, covered in orange oilcloth and topped with paper place mats. The menu is scribbled on blackboards and paper plates tacked to the wall. You can order the plat du jour and a carafe of the house red, and get away with spending less than $10 for a filling and satisfying meal of roast chicken, pork, duck, or veal, all garnished with more than enough potatoes. For dessert, splurge on a slice of the fresh fruit *tarte* which is made daily in the lilliputian kitchen in the back.

MÉTRO
4-Septembre

OPEN
Mon–Fri lunch only

CLOSED
Dinner; Sat, Sun; holidays; Aug

HOURS
Lunch noon–2:45 P.M.

RESERVATIONS
No

CREDIT CARDS
None

A LA CARTE
35–50F, BNC

PRIX FIXE
41F, 1 entree and cheese or dessert, BNC; 61F, 3 courses, wine and coffee included

L'Amanguier
110, rue de Richelieu (2nd)

Trendy restaurants come and go every day in Paris, but L'Amanguier lasts because it has a formula that works: efficient service, reasonable prices, and good food served seven days a week in pleasant garden settings. It's true that it's a chain, but there are very few restaurants in this price category that offer such consistent quality in both food and service. The crowd in all four locations mixes cute young things in tight jeans with grandes dames in furs and successful businessmen in power suits.

The menu offers a wealth of appealing selections and an ever-changing list of seasonal specialties. For dessert, let your cautionary wall down and order one of the fantasy pastries or frosty ice cream creations made in their in-house bakery, Le Framboisier.

TELEPHONE
42-96-37-79

MÉTRO
Richelieu-Drouot

OPEN
Daily lunch and dinner

CLOSED
May 1; NAC

HOURS
Lunch noon–2:30 P.M., Dinner 7–midnight

RESERVATIONS
Yes on weekends and holidays

CREDIT CARDS
AE, DC, MC, V

A LA CARTE
135F, BNC

PRIX FIXE
110F, 3 courses, BC

La Patata
25, boulevard des Italiens (2nd)

For more food than you can probably eat in one sitting, drop in anytime at La Patata, Patrick Namura's newest gourmet potato restaurant. La Patata serves baked potatoes topped with a variety of

TELEPHONE
42-68-16-66

MÉTRO
Richelieu-Drouot

OPEN
Daily

CLOSED
Never; NAC

HOURS
11 A.M.–midnight,
continuous service

RESERVATIONS
No

CREDIT CARDS
V

A LA CARTE
70–100F, BNC

PRIX FIXE
None

ingredients, on square platters garnished with salad and cheese or fresh fruit. To ease the pangs of dieters, the *carte* states the calorie equivalents of 100 g of bread (250) and 100 g of baked potato (80).

There is something here for every taste. Starting with the child's portion (12 years and younger), diners can select from 14 combinations. The Patata Mexicaine comes with chili con carne and guacamole; the Patata Montagnarde has *raclette*, ham, tomatoes, pickles, and onions; and the Patata Californienne is topped with hamburger, ketchup, onions, cheese, and corn.

Tipping the dessert scales are huge sundaes and the amazing Banana Patata: a big dish overflowing with maple walnut and vanilla ice cream, surrounded by hot chocolate and whipped cream, with an entire banana under it all.

Le Vaudeville
29, rue Vivienne (2nd)

TELEPHONE
40-20-04-62

MÉTRO
Bourse

OPEN
Daily lunch and dinner

CLOSED
Never; NAC

HOURS
Lunch noon–3:30 P.M.,
dinner 7 P.M.–2 A.M.

RESERVATIONS
Yes

CREDIT CARDS
AE, DC, MC, V

A LA CARTE
170F, BNC

PRIX FIXE
None

A polished crowd of locals and out-of-towners drifts into Jean-Paul Bucher's 1920s-style *brasserie* for the pleasure of meeting and eating. At lunch, you will share your meal with stockbrokers and commodity traders from the nearby Bourse. In the evening, the sophisticated set arrives about 10 P.M. in anything from black tie and satin to pastel pullovers and athletic shoes. Formally clad waiters serve without keeping anyone waiting too long or making it seem as though they're overworked during the peak hours. On a warm day, the coveted terrace tables are a great place to sit and soak up the street scene, as you delve into familiar dishes ordered from a vast menu that changes daily and even lists the plat du jour for the following day.

This is the sort of place where it is easy to get carried away and spend too much money. If you choose wisely and order the dry house Riesling wine, however, your bill shouldn't be too astounding.

Lina's Sandwiches
50, rue Étienne-Marcel (2nd)

When I am in the neighborhood and need a fast lunch, Lina's is my Cheap Eat destination. Big, bright, and new on the Paris scene, they offer minimal decor and fantastic sandwiches to the many lunch-bunchers who line up for their orders to go, or to eat there. Rather than stand up at one of the tables, I head for a stool along the window counter to indulge in first-class people-watching between bites.

All the sandwiches are made to order on additive-free whole-meal bread or rolls and run the gamut from egg salad to smoked salmon. Box lunches with six different sandwich selections are available, and so are soups, salads, and some of the richest brownies in Paris.

TELEPHONE
42-21-16-14
MÉTRO
Étienne-Marcel
OPEN
Mon–Fri
CLOSED
Sat, Sun; holidays; NAC
HOURS
Mon–Fri 9 A.M.–7 P.M., continuous service
RESERVATIONS
No
CREDIT CARDS
V
A LA CARTE
35–65F, BC
PRIX FIXE
Box lunches: 210F–220F, 6 varieties

Matinée-Soirée
5, rue Marie Stuart (2nd)

Some of the best-priced Parisian eating places are buried in the most out-of-the-way back streets. Matinée-Soirée is no exception. It is a little hard to find, but if you study your *Plan de Paris* map of the 2nd arrondissement, you won't regret the effort. Situated on a dreary side street no tourist would ever stroll down on purpose, this *restaurant de quartier par excellence* was introduced to me by friends who count themselves among its many loyal followers. It is an informal spot; if you appear here in a coat and tie you will be branded a tourist. The plain interior consists of orange linen napkins on paper table covers, a green plant or two, and candles at night. The tasty, well-made, and pleasantly served food is the reason Matinée-Soirée is packed every night when others in the area are half full. At lunch, the ambience is bright, with efficient service making possible a quick, three-course lunch with wine for under $15. In the evening, it doesn't get going until 9:30 or 10 P.M., when there isn't an empty table, even on Monday nights. The small menu features seasonal suggestions as well as

TELEPHONE
42-21-18-00
MÉTRO
Étienne-Marcel
OPEN
Mon–Fri lunch and dinner, Sat dinner only
CLOSED
Sat lunch, Sun; holidays; Aug
HOURS
Lunch noon–2 P.M., dinner 8–11:30 P.M.
RESERVATIONS
Advised on weekends
CREDIT CARDS
MC, V
A LA CARTE
130F, BNC
PRIX FIXE
Lunch: 62F, 3 courses, BC; dinner 85F, 3 courses, BNC, and 145F, 3 courses, BNC

some that are always available. I like to start with the salad of *chèvre chaud* and hope that they will have either the leg of lamb or fillet of sole for the main course. Always on the menu, and without question the best I have ever tasted, is the *crème brûlée*, lightly flavored with citrus and flambéed with Grand Mariner. Just thinking about it makes my mouth water.

THIRD ARRONDISSEMENT

Marais means "swamp" in French, and it was just that until the 14th century when it became a royal park. Today, a walk through this area is a lesson in the history of French domestic architecture. The area has been redeveloped with panache, and many of the 17th- and 18th-century buildings have been made into museums or returned to their former glory as sumptuous apartments. This heaven for walkers and wanderers of all types is full of shops, boutiques, appealing restaurants, and fascinating history.

THIRD ARRONDISSEMENT
Right Bank: Carnavalet Museum (the museum of the city of Paris), French National Archives, Marais, Picasso Museum

THIRD ARRONDISSEMENT RESTAURANTS

Batifol
Café de la Cité

Chez Jenny
L'Ambassade d'Auvergne

Batifol
15, place de la République (3rd)
Telephone: 42-77-86-88
Métro: République
Hours: 11 A.M.–2 A.M., dinner 6:30–10:30 P.M.

See page 35.

Café de la Cité
22, rue Rambuteau (3rd)

You will find this cozy little Cheap Eats discovery sandwiched between a horse butcher and a flower stall on one of the few remaining *marché* streets in the area, just minutes away from all the hoopla around Beaubourg and Les Halles.

With its daily specials carefully handwritten on blackboards hanging both inside and outside, this little hole-in-the-wall café always packs them in, especially at lunch, when all the seats are taken by 12:15, and the crowd often overflows onto the sidewalk and into the street.

The food isn't sophisticated, and you won't be sampling exotic sauces or wild game. You will, how-

TELEPHONE
42-78-56-36
MÉTRO
Rambuteau
OPEN
Mon–Sat breakfast, lunch, and dinner
CLOSED
Sun; NAC
HOURS
Breakfast (Continental only) 8–11:30 A.M., lunch noon–4 P.M., dinner 7–11:30 P.M.
RESERVATIONS
Not accepted for lunch; not necessary for dinner
CREDIT CARDS
None

A LA CARTE
None
PRIX FIXE
Lunch: all *entrées* 15F, all *plats*
39–49F, all desserts 15F; dinner: 1 *entrée* and 1 *plat* 60F, 1
plat 47F, all desserts 15F, BNC

ever, be eating old-fashioned back-burner-style
French cooking and plenty of it, all for a great low
price, while surrounded by coveralled construction
workers, young professionals, local artists, and neighborhood regulars doing the same thing.

Chez Jenny
39, boulevard du Temple (3rd)

TELEPHONE
42-74-75-75
MÉTRO
République
OPEN
Daily
CLOSED
Never; NAC
HOURS
11:30 A.M–1:30 A.M.;
continuous service
RESERVATIONS
Not necessary, except for
downstairs seats
CREDIT CARDS
AE, DC, MC, V
A LA CARTE
130F, BNC (includes wine
and coffee)
PRIX FIXE
150F, 3 courses, BNC;
12 years and under: 80F, 3
courses, BNC

Chez Jenny celebrates the food and wine of Alsace,
served in a magnificent old brasserie full of fabulous
regional artwork. Rosy-cheeked waitresses wearing
starched headdresses and dirndls serve the brimming
plates and offer helpful advice with the menus, which
are in French, German, and English.

If you are looking for some of the best *choucroute*
in Paris, look no farther; head to Chez Jenny to lap
up steaming platters of smoked slab bacon, bratwurst,
plump white veal sausages, lean smoked pork loin,
savory sauerkraut, and a stein of golden beer. For a
lighter supper, order the assorted *charcuterie* of mild
Alsatian sausages, or a *plat* of iced oysters and shellfish with a glass of chilled Riesling wine. (Warning:
Do not order the strange fish *choucroute*.) You probably won't be in the mood for dessert after all this,
but if you can possibly squeeze it in, have the *gâteau
au fromage blanc* (cheesecake), their specialty.

The cavernous interior is as impressive as the food:
carved wall plaques, life-size wooden figures in native
dress, and lovely murals depicting life in the colorful
Alsatian region of France along the German border.
For the best overall atmosphere, reserve a table on
the ground floor.

L'Ambassade d'Auvergne
22, rue de Grenier St-Lazare (3rd)

TELEPHONE
42-72-31-22
MÉTRO
Rambuteau,
rue du Grenier-St-Lazare exit

Nicole and Bernard Areny and Francis Moulier,
the owners of L'Ambassade d'Auvergne, regard themselves as culinary representatives of their native region. Over the years, their restaurant has remained
true to its heritage and is today one of the finest

regional restaurants in Paris. On the many times I have eaten here, I have always found all the elements of the restaurant working together to create a satisfying dining experience. There are six dining rooms and a clientele that includes prominent political figures. For the most authentic and beautiful atmosphere, reserve a table downstairs, which has an open fireplace and massive beams hung with hundreds of Auvergne hams.

Country abundance is evident in every delicious dish, from the specials that remain the same each day of the week to the seasonal offerings. A wonderful *entrée* anytime is the cabbage soup with white beans, ham chunks, potatoes, carrots, and Roquefort cheese. Tempting main dishes are the spicy Auvergne sausages with lentils, *la falette* (a stuffed boned breast of veal in an herb sauce), and, for the adventurous, the *tripous à l'estragon* (tripe). An absolute *must* with whatever you order is *l'aligot*, a masterful blend of puréed potatoes and melted Cantal cheese, whipped at your table and served from copper pans. Trying to save room for dessert is difficult, but if you can, they are delicately delicious, especially the creamy chocolate mousse served from a crystal bowl, or the *assiette des desserts d'Auvergne*, bite-sized samplings of their most popular selections.

OPEN
Daily lunch and dinner

CLOSED
Never; NAC

HOURS
Lunch noon–2:30 P.M., dinner 7:30–11:30 P.M.

RESERVATIONS
Yes

CREDIT CARDS
MC, V

A LA CARTE
190F, BNC

PRIX FIXE
None

FOURTH ARRONDISSEMENT

Point zero is a compass rose set in the pavement in front of Notre-Dame Cathedral. This is the spot from which all distances are measured in France, but more than that, it is the spiritual, emotional, and administrative heart of France. The Île St-Louis, with 6,000 inhabitants and a village spirit, is a small microcosm of Paris. Full of atmosphere, the narrow streets house beautiful *hotel particulières* (private mansions) occupied by famous film stars, authors, the Rothschilds, and many expatriots. In the Marais, the Place des Vosges is considered the most beautiful square in Paris. It was an up-and-coming area; now it has arrived. Young fashion designers fight for shop space, and rents are astronomical. The famous fashion houses on the Rue du Faubourg St-Honoré and Avenue Montaigne are for rich Japanese and American tourists; stylish young French men and women shop in the Marais for the latest word in clothes. This part of the Marais is also the center of the Parisian Jewish community. Take a stroll down Rue des Rosiers and discover tempting kosher delicatessens and restaurants. While you are in the fourth, you can visit the museum of modern art, better known as the Centre Georges Pompidou, or Beaubourg, and now the number-one tourist attraction in Paris, surpassing the Eiffel Tower and the Louvre Museum in its number of visitors per year.

FOURTH ARRONDISSEMENT RESTAURANTS

Auberge de Jarente	Les Philosophes
Au Gourmet de l'Île	Lt Temps des Cerises
Au Petit Fer à Cheval	L'Excuse
Bofinger	L'Oulette
Brasserie de l'Île St-Louis	Mariage Frères
	Nos Ancêtres les Gaulois
Brasserie Ma Bourgogne	San Francisco Muffin
Chez Julien	Company
Le Relais de l'Isle	Trumilou

Auberge de Jarente
7, rue de Jarente (4th)

It is not much from the outside, or from the inside either, for that matter, but what counts is the food, and it is *good*. This two-room *auberge* on the edge of the Marais specializes in Basque dishes from southwestern France. If you order the prix fixe menu, you will have some difficult dining decisions ahead. Should you try the *pipérade*, a mixture of sweet red bell peppers, tomatoes, onions, and garlic mixed with scrambled eggs and topped with spicy sausage? Or would a big bowl of fish soup or the frog's legs be a better beginning? For the main course, should you call ahead and order the paella (24 hours in advance), or should you have the *confit de canard*, the *cassoulet*, or the *cailles à la façon du chef*: two highly flavored quail served with perfectly sautéed potatoes? For dessert, the best choice far and away is their version of *gâteau Basque*, a cream-filled cake. For the nicest experience of the restaurant, arrive about 9 or 9:30 P.M. when the French do, order a bottle of the Madiran red wine, and settle into a full-flavored meal that won't put a major strain on your budget.

TELEPHONE
42-77-49-35

MÉTRO
St-Paul or Bastille

OPEN
Tues–Sat lunch and dinner

CLOSED
Sun, Mon; major holidays, Aug 5–Sept 5; 1st week of April, 1 week at Christmas

HOURS
Lunch noon–2:30 P.M., dinner 7:30–10:30 P.M.

RESERVATIONS
For lunch and after 8:30 P.M.

CREDIT CARDS
AE, DC, MC, V

A LA CARTE
155F, BNC

PRIX FIXE
106F, 4 courses, BNC; 120F, 4 courses, BC

Au Gourmet de l'Île
42, rue St-Louis-en-l'Île (4th)

One of the best value-for-money meals in Paris can be found at this rustic 17th-century beamed and candlelit restaurant on the Île St-Louis. I worried when it was sold by its longtime owner, Jules Bordeau. I needn't have. The new proprietors, M. and Mme. Jourdin, are on their toes and continue to reflect Bordeau's love of good-quality food and service. Diners can be assured of finding expert versions of simple French country classics served in a friendly, crowded atmosphere. A warning is in order, however, because most of the food served here in not for those with tame tastes.

In the window is a sign reading "A.A.A.A.A.," which stands for the Amiable Association of Ama-

TELEPHONE
43-26-79-27

MÉTRO
Pont-Marie

OPEN
Tues, Wed, Fri–Sun lunch and dinner

CLOSED
Mon, Thurs; Aug

HOURS
Lunch noon–2 P.M., dinner 7–10 P.M.

RESERVATIONS
Essential for dinner and Sun

CREDIT CARDS
MC, V

A LA CARTE
135F, BNC
PRIX FIXE
120F, 4 courses, BNC

teurs of the Authentic Andouillette. If you have never tried one of these French soul-food sausages made with chitterlings, now is the time. This is also the place to sample such French standards as *cervelles* (brains), *boudin* (blood sausage), *rognons* (kidneys), and *ris d'agneau* (lamb kidneys).

Those with more timid palates will enjoy the other house specialties of grilled guinea hen with lentils, and the filling *la carbonnèe de l'Île*, a robust pork stew in red wine with bacon, onions, potatoes, and croutons. Everyone will love the desserts, especially the *crème limousine*, a caramel custard swimming in warm chocolate sauce.

Au Petit Fer à Cheval
30, rue Vieille du Temple (4th)

TELEPHONE
42-72-47-47
MÉTRO
Hôtel-de-Ville, St-Paul le-Marais
OPEN
Daily
CLOSED
Never; NAC
HOURS
Noon–midnight, continuous service
RESERVATIONS
No
CREDIT CARDS
None
A LA CARTE
Lunch and dinner: 85F–110F, BNC
PRIX FIXE
None

Cheap, cheerful, basic, and truly French—that's Au Petit Fer à Cheval, a popular hub for everyone from shopkeepers and stray tourists to new wave patrons just in from Pluto.

This slightly seedy Marais landmark consists of sidewalk tables, a marble-topped horseshoe bar in the front room, and a larger room in the back to handle the overflow. You can stop by anytime for a quick *café express* at the bar, or sit down and consume a home-cooked lunch or dinner.

Expect to find salads, steaks, daily *plats*, and old dessert standards such as chocolate mousse and floating island. While the food isn't anything to entice a line of gourmet diners, it is filling and typical of what the natives thrive on.

Bofinger
5–7, rue de la Bastille (4th)

TELEPHONE
42-72-87-82
MÉTRO
Bastille
OPEN
Daily, lunch and dinner

What better way to spend the evening than in the company of friends, enjoying good food and wine, in the oldest and most handsome brasserie in Paris, located only a few minutes from the stunning new opera house at Place de la Bastille? While not the place for a romantic tête-à-tête, you can't help feeling glamorous and festive when dining at Bofinger. The magnificent Belle Époque decor on two floors, with its maze of mirrors, brass, stained glass, and flowers, provides the perfect backdrop for the see-and-be-seen crowds of fashionable French who flock here every night. Do not even *think* of arriving without a reservation. While culinary fireworks are not the order of the day, the food is good, and the copious servings cater to healthy appetites. Platters of oysters, traditional *choucroutes*, and grilled meats lead the list of the best dining choices. The house Riesling is a good wine selection. The service, by black-tied waiters who sometimes ferry plates over the heads of diners, is swift and accurate. *Note:* Women should not miss seeing the opulent ladies' room.

CLOSED
Never; NAC

HOURS
Lunch noon–3 P.M., dinner 7:30 P.M.–1 A.M.

RESERVATIONS
Essential

CREDIT CARDS
AE, DC, MC, V

A LA CARTE
200F, BNC

PRIX FIXE
160F, 3 courses, BC

Brasserie de l'Île St-Louis
55, quai de Bourbon (4th)

A stroll over the pedestrian bridge behind Notre-Dame to the Île St-Louis brings you right to the doorstep of this picturesque old *auberge*, which has become a favorite watering hole and gathering place for many of the writers, entertainers, and expatriates who live on the island. The atmosphere is bustling, colorful, and very friendly. It is impossible to feel lonely here for long.

Aside from all this, the food is good and the prices are low. The menu features typical brasserie dishes as well as Alsatian specialties of pickled pigs' feet, spicy sausages, *cassoulet*, and creamy onion tarts washed down with pitchers of house white wine or mugs of frothy beer. Desserts tend to be uninspiring. Instead, walk down the center street of the island to the Berthillon ice cream shop (31, rue St-Louis-en-l'Île) and treat yourself to several scoops of their famous ice cream or *sorbet*.

TELEPHONE
43-54-02-59

MÉTRO
Pont-Marie

OPEN
Fri–Tues

CLOSED
Wed, Thurs; Feb school vacations; Aug

HOURS
11:30 A.M.–2 A.M., continuous service

RESERVATIONS
No

CREDIT CARDS
None

A LA CARTE
140F, BNC

PRIX FIXE
None

Brasserie Ma Bourgogne
19, place des Vosges (4th)

Ma Bourgogne has been immortalized by the au-

TELEPHONE
42-78-44-64

PRIX FIXE
Weekends only: 170F,
3 courses (choice of any *entrée*,
plat, and dessert from menu),
BNC

thor Georges Simenon as one of the places frequented by Inspector Maigret. It is not surprising that Simenon would choose this classic brasserie situated on the historic Place des Vosges. The best seats are outside at the wicker tables closely placed beneath the 17th-century arcade, facing the park and surrounded by the lovely sandstone and pink brick buildings that form the oldest square in Paris.

Try it any time of day for the experience of mixing with Parisians in one of their favorite places. Go for breakfast to watch the early-morning flow of life in the Marais: taxi drivers double-parking to grab a quick espresso; singles on their way to work; an old man and his grandson, a heavy book bag on the boy's back, having a croissant and hot chocolate before school. At lunch and dinner it is crowded with locals pitching into daily specials of traditional food and drinking the modestly priced Burgundy, Beaujolais, and Loire wines. In the afternoon, it is pleasant and peaceful to sit outside, sip a cool drink, and watch fashionable people strolling by as they browse through the many antique shops and art galleries located under the arcades. In the evening, Ma Bourgogne radiates a quiet good cheer with its clientele of stylishly turned-out neighborhood Parisians enjoying one of the regional specialties or the famed steak *tartare.*

Chez Julien
Corner of 1, rue Pont-Louis-Philippe, and 62, rue de l'Hôtel-de-Ville (4th)

OPEN
Mon dinner only, Tues–Sat
lunch and dinner

The days of leisurely dining, polished service, and good taste live on at Chez Julien. Located on a picturesque square along the Seine, this former 19th-century bakery and now historical monument retains its original classic façade, antique windows, and magnificent painted glass ceilings. Its opulent beauty has not been lost on French or American film directors, who have shot many a Parisian restaurant scene here. One of the most noteworthy was *The Accidental*

Tourist, with William Hurt enjoying his dinner by an open window with a view across the Seine to the tip of the l'Île St-Louis.

The *nouvelle cuisine* vies with the interior for richness and virtuosity. For the *entrée*, the *profiteroles d' escargots* with garlic butter or the nest of *tagliatelle* flavored with basil is a memorable choice. The simple *filet de boeuf* with an intriguing five-pepper sauce, the boneless duck breast in a fresh orange sauce, and the salmon with watercress sauce are stellar main courses. The desserts include four fruit *sorbets* in a whimsical cookie crust, and plump prunes drenched in Tia Maria. The pièce de résistance, however, is the *succès au chocolat*, an almost illegally rich chocolate dessert made with sponge cake, layered with rich chocolate mousse, covered with dark-chocolate frosting, and surrounded by a coffee sauce. Absolutely a little taste of heaven. Complimentary pastries served with a *café express* make a fitting finale to the evening. Prices are on the high side, so reserve this dining pleasure for special occasions, or just to celebrate being in Paris.

Note: When reserving, ask to be seated in the main room, not in the area where you enter the restaurant, and most certainly *never* upstairs.

RESERVATIONS
Yes

CREDIT CARDS
MC, V

A LA CARTE
250F, BNC

PRIX FIXE
Lunch only: 140F,
3 courses, BNC

Le Relais de l'Isle
37, rue St-Louis-en-l'Île (4th)

I discovered Pascal Hardel's restaurant while on my way to another that ultimately fell into the pile of rejects. I was charmed by the beamed ceilings and rustic decor in this tiny spot that reflects the old-world atmosphere on the popular Île St-Louis. A romantic note is added in the evening when the candles glow and a pianist often plays. I was also impressed by the animated diners who were obviously enjoying their meals.

The cuisine consists of a simple repertoire of fresh, top-quality products served in generous portions from a prix fixe menu only. For a dependable appetizer, order the salad topped with slices of smoked duck, or

TELEPHONE
46-34-72-34

MÉTRO
Pont-Marie

OPEN
Thurs–Mon, lunch and dinner,
Wed dinner only

CLOSED
Tues all day, Wed lunch;
major holidays; Jan 15–Feb 15

HOURS
Lunch noon–2:30 P.M.,
dinner 7–10:30 P.M.

RESERVATIONS
Yes

CREDIT CARDS
AE, DC, MC, V
A LA CARTE
None
PRIX FIXE
Lunch: 55F, *entrée* and *plat*,,
BNC; dinner: 140F, 3 courses,
BNC

the briney fish soup. The best main courses are the fricassée of chicken cooked in cider and served with fresh noodles, and the grilled lamb chops with potatoes *dauphinois* and tomatoes *provençale*. The desserts are all good, but the best are made with the homemade ice cream.

After eating here, I must agree with my dinner companion who said, "For food like this at home, people would line up around the block and pay twice as much."

Les Philosophes
28, rue Vielle-du-Temple (4th)

TELEPHONE
48-87-49-64
MÉTRO
St-Paul, Hôtel-de-Ville
OPEN
Mon–Sat, lunch and dinner
CLOSED
Sun, 1 week at Christmas,
4 days around May 1; Aug
HOURS
Lunch noon–2 P.M.,
dinner 7:30–11 P.M.
RESERVATIONS
Yes
CREDIT CARDS
AE, MC, V
A LA CARTE
170F, BNC
PRIX FIXE
72F, 2 courses (*entrée* and *plat*),
BNC; 85F, 3 courses, BNC;
118F, 3 courses, BNC

It is a joy to find this perfect little *quartier* restaurant so unchanged over the years. The formal dining room, framed by lacy window curtains, displays fresh flower bouquets, starched linen on the tables, and a tiny corner bar. The traditional menu has something to appeal to everyone, the specialties are excellent, and the prices are right: three solid reasons why residents who want to share a few hours over a nice meal with a bottle of good wine and not spend outrageously doing so reserve a table here. The prix fixe menus display a range of classic cuisine that is carefully prepared with the best fresh ingredients. You can expect to find such timeless favorites as duck *terrine*, sole *meunière*, medallions of *lotte* in a light fennel sauce, *boeuf Stroganoff,* and a tantalizing hot apple *tarte* that must be ordered at the start of the meal. Tempting those with more adventurous minds are the steak *tartare*, liver and bacon in a light cream sauce, and a fine *andouillette*. If you order from one of the set menus and complement your meal with a pitcher or a bottle of an inexpensive little wine, your bill should add up to much less than you would pay for the same fare at home.

Le Temps des Cerises
31, rue de la Cerisaie (4th)

Le Temps des Cerises is the place to have a cheap

meal while polishing your fractured French. When you arrive, you won't miss owner Gerard, with his handlebar mustache, standing behind the bar, pouring drinks for the regulars and teasing all the women. Lunch is the liveliest time here, attracting a relatively young neighborhood clientele who seem to accept the crowded conditions in order to enjoy the kind of honest home cooking that Mother never has time to make anymore. The three prix fixe lunch menus read like a textbook and include all the basics, from Auvergne sausage to yogurt. Wines run from 19F for the house varieties to 250F for a *grand cru* of Bordeaux. Naturally, this is the place to down a pitcher or two of the house red and save the *grand cru* for another day.

Before and after the hectic lunch scene, the café is calm, with the old-timers standing at the bar dusting off memories about times gone by. No one speaks much English, and you might have to share a table or elbow your way to a space at the bar, but go ahead, don't be shy. Everyone is friendly, and new faces are welcome.

TELEPHONE
42-72-08-63

MÉTRO
Sully-Morland, Bastille

OPEN
Mon–Fri, bar and lunch

CLOSED
Dinner; Sat, Sun; holidays; Aug

HOURS
Bar 7:30 A.M.–8 P.M., lunch 11:30 A.M.–2:30 P.M.

RESERVATIONS
No

CREDIT CARDS
None

A LA CARTE
None

PRIX FIXE
55F, 3 courses, BNC

L'Excuse
14, rue Charles-V (4th)

There is an elegant glow to the little bar and two dining rooms, which are tastefully decorated with soft lighting, fresh flowers, and attractive posters. Correctly set, reasonably well-spaced tables preserve a sense of intimacy, and the strains of classical music enhance the sophisticated mood, making L'Excuse a perfect choice for *le dîner à deux.*

Owner Jean-Denis Barbet is on hand daily to make sure no details go unnoticed or unattended. Throughout the year, his chef creates four seasonally innovative menus. In the spring, worthy starters might include a warm, flaky pastry filled with asparagus purée, and surrounded by a chervil wine sauce, or an avocado and grapefruit salad with two types of imported ham. Heading the list of main courses are

TELEPHONE
42-77-98-97

MÉTRO
St-Paul

OPEN
Mon–Sat, lunch and dinner

CLOSED
Sun; major holidays; NAC

HOURS
Lunch noon–2 P.M., dinner 7:30–11 P.M.

RESERVATIONS
Essential

CREDIT CARDS
V

A LA CARTE
240F, BNC

PRIX FIXE
145F, 3 courses, BNC

the lamb chops garnished with fresh vegetables, and an unusual fillet of pork marinated in a mixture of coconut milk, white wine, and juniper berries. Light desserts to please anyone are the brochettes of fresh fruit flambéed in Cointreau, and the *crème brûlée* served with *financiers* (little sponge-cake fingers). In the eight years it has been open, L'Excuse has developed a dedicated following, which makes reservations essential. In whatever season you go, you will have an exquisite meal and enjoy impeccable service.

L'Oulette
38, rue des Tournelles (4th)

TELEPHONE
42-71-43-33

MÉTRO
Bastille

OPEN
Mon–Fri, lunch and dinner

CLOSED
Sat, Sun; holidays; a few days around May 1; 3 weeks in Aug; 1 week at Christmas

HOURS
Lunch noon–2 P.M., dinner 8–10 P.M.

RESERVATIONS
Absolutely essential, as far in advance as possible

CREDIT CARDS
MC, V

A LA CARTE
200–215F, BNC

PRIX FIXE
Lunch: 120F, 3 courses, BNC; dinner: 150F, 3 courses, BNC

If you have time for only one special meal in Paris, L'Oulette tops my short list of recommendations. Chef Marcel Baudis and his wife Marie-Noëlle opened their little bistro featuring dishes from Quercy in the southwestern part of France only a few years ago. Since then, it has been discovered by *toute le monde* and has become one of the most difficult of places to book. Reservations are now absolutely essential at least a week in advance.

Chef Baudis spends hours in his tiny kitchen preparing his dishes, which are meticulously arranged and politely presented by Marie-Noëlle and one other server. Meals like this cannot be rushed, so plan an evening of sitting back, enjoying a good bottle of wine, and savoring a truly outstanding meal.

Expect delicate perfection from the talented hands in the kitchen with such innovative dishes as guinea fowl stuffed with mushrooms, braised oxtails and pigs' feet in a hearty red wine sauce, veal tongue with saffron and mushrooms, and tender lamb medallions seasoned with cumin and garnished with an array of garden vegetables. For dessert, do no miss the hot, flaky fruit *tourtière*, which you must order at the beginning of your meal. There's really nothing more to say, except that L'Oulette is a dining treat you should have.

Mariage Frères
30–32, rue de Bourg-Tibourg (4th)

No serious tea-lover can afford to miss the Tiffany of teahouses in Paris: Mariage Frères, which has been dedicated for more than 130 years to the art of tea drinking. Over 350 teas from 25 countries are prepared in these world-famous shops by master tea makers who still do everything by hand, including carefully cutting and stitching each tea bag out of tissue or muslin.

The ambience is an important part of the experience of drinking tea here. You are encouraged to taste teas at brunch, lunch, or afternoon tea while listening to classical music. Knowledgeable white-coated waiters suggest the appropriate tea to drink with each meal. As the menu states, "Tea is not all in the pot." Many of the dishes are prepared *with* tea, from jams and jellies to sauces, ice creams, and *sorbets*. The food is all good; the tea, of course, is beyond reproach; and the prices are slightly high, but well worth it for the lovely experience.

In conjunction with the tearoom on Rue du Bourg-Tibourg, there is a wonderful tea shop, with the original cash box used in the first tea shop, and a small tea museum. The newest location on Rue des Grands-Augustins doesn't have the wide range of teas and tea accessories to buy, but the food and refined service are just the same. At both locations, patrons are requested not to smoke.

TELEPHONE
42-72-28-11

MÉTRO
Hôtel-de-Ville

OPEN
Tues–Sun

CLOSED
Mon; NAC

HOURS
Teashop 10:30 A.M.–7:30 P.M., brunch Sat and Sun noon–6 P.M., lunch noon–3 P.M. (the restaurant will not serve just tea and pastry during this time); tea 3–7 P.M.

RESERVATIONS
Advised on weekends

CREDIT CARDS
AE, MC, V

A LA CARTE
130–150F, BC

PRIX FIXE
Sat and Sun brunch: 150F, BC and 185F, BC; anytime brunch: 120F, BC

Nos Ancêtres les Gaulois
39, rue St-Louis-en-l'Île (4th)

"Our Ancestors the Gauls" promises raucous fun and all-you-can-eat farm food in beamed and vaulted rooms at trestle tables for 2 or 20. Up to 300 revelers can be served each night by the tireless waiters, who wear tunic vests made from clipped brown and white fur. All of this is presided over by the general factotum, Lucien, or "Lulu," as he prefers to be called. Dressed like an ancient Gaul, he stomps around the

TELEPHONE
46-33-66-07, 46-33-66-12

MÉTRO
Pont-Marie

OPEN
Nightly for dinner; Sun lunch; holidays for lunch

CLOSED
Lunch Mon–Sat; NAC

dining room coercing his guests to make gluttons of themselves.

You start by munching on loaves of dark country bread, cold meats, and raw vegetables, and help yourself to the salad buffet while waiting for your choice of main dishes, which include steaks, lamb chops, or shish kebabs grilled over an open fire. The main course is followed by great platters of cheeses and a choice of three desserts. As much red wine as you can drink, served from a huge cask at the center of the restaurant, is included in the price of the meal.

While gorging yourself and drinking quantities of wine may not be what you have in mind for a romantic evening, this is a great place to unwind with a group and have a Rabelaisian feast you will long remember.

San Francisco Muffin Company
67, rue Rambuteau (4th)

Hats off to Linda Rossi-Koblentz for having the insight to start the San Francisco Muffin Company in Paris. Banking on the Parisian's fascination with most things American, she opened her first shop to rave reviews and long lines of hungry French people eager to sample the comfortingly familiar taste of American food. All day long, the tiny storefront counters sell takeout orders of banana bread, carrot cake, blueberry, corn, and bran muffins, cookies, brownies, club sandwiches, BLT's, frozen yogurt, and cheesecake. If you need more of an American food fix, this is the only place in Paris where you can purchase Orville Redenbacker's popcorn, Thomas Brothers English Muffins, H&H Bagels, and Jiffy chunky peanut butter.

Trumilou
84, quai de l'Hôtel-de-Ville (4th)

It's a bar, a bistro, or a restaurant, depending on where you sit in this Cheap Eats jewel located in a 16th-century building along the Seine and run by the Dumond family who also own La Poule au Pot (see page 101). For years Trumilou has been rewarding artists, writers, students, and many other devotées with low tabs, good service, and sensible food that has survived the changing times, trends, and food crazes rolling through Paris. The regulars know enough to go early for both lunch and dinner to avoid the crowds that build up as the mealtime wears on.

The decor is minimal, yet the place radiates an authentic atmosphere. It doesn't matter whether you eat in the large main room crowded with tables for two or four; in the slightly smaller, more intimate room with vases of flowers and crystal chandeliers; next to the bar and the pinball machine; or on the sidewalk terrace. The only concern here is the food, which brings happy diners back time after time.

MÉTRO
Hôtel-de-Ville, Pont-Marie

OPEN
Tues–Sun lunch, dinner, and bar

CLOSED
Mon; Christmas; NAC

HOURS
Bar 8 A.M.–1 A.M., lunch noon–3 P.M., dinner 7–11 P.M.

RESERVATIONS
For groups

CREDIT CARDS
V

A LA CARTE
100F, BC

PRIX FIXE
58F, BNC; 76F, BNC

FIFTH ARRONDISSEMENT

FIFTH ARRONDISSEMENT
Left Bank: Cluny Museum (art of the Middle Ages), Jardin des Plantes, Latin Quarter, Rue Mouffetard, Panthéon, Sorbonne.

Since medieval days, this area has been the student *quartier* of Paris. Associated with perpetual youth, intellectuals, artists, writers, poets, and a bohemian lifestyle, the area is dotted with restaurants, cafés, bars, bookstores, and movie theaters. Many of the eating places are nothing more than greasy spoons, especially along Rue de la Harpe and Rue de la Huchette.

A visit to one of the most colorful markets in Paris, Rue Mouffetard, is a must. The market is open Tuesday through Sunday from 8 A.M. to 1 P.M., and is overflowing with every kind of food imaginable, clothing shops, little cafés, and a fascinating parade of people.

FIFTH ARRONDISSEMENT RESTAURANTS

Au Bistro de la
  Sorbonne
Au Buisson Ardent
Brasserie Balzar
Jardin des Pâtes
La Fontaine Saint-
  Victor
La Petite Légume
La Rôtisserie du
  Beaujolais
L'Assiette aux
  Fromages

Le Baptiste
Le Berthoud
Le Bistro d'Hannah
Le Grenier de Notre-
  Dame
Le Mouffetard
Le Raccard
Le Vieux Chêne
Moissonnier
Perraudin
Restaurant Chez Marius

Au Bistro de la Sorbonne
4, rue Toullier (5th)

TELEPHONE
43-54-41-49
MÉTRO
Luxembourg
OPEN
Mon–Sat lunch and dinner
CLOSED
Sun; holidays; NAC

Look for an orange sign with a No. 4 on Rue Toullier, just off Rue Soufflot near the Sorbonne. Any time you go, it is likely to be filled with a cross-section of people, ranging from young couples holding hands, to secretaries and their bosses, or families in from the provinces who appreciate a filling meal.

All hungry Cheap Eaters will get plenty for their money here, especially if they stick to the prix fixe menu, which includes an all-you-can-eat buffet of cold *entrées*. Diners are encouraged to pile their plates high with helpings of marinated vegetables, sausage, and *terrines*, cabbage and potato salads, *céleri rémoulade*, *tarama*, and much more. As a main course, the steaks and brochettes of lamb or pork are bound to win the hearts of all meat eaters. Lighter appetites will enjoy the ham, cheese, and egg crêpe, and the *délice de la Sorbonne* (chicken, ham, and spinach in a cream sauce with a cheese topping). Desserts tend to be uninspired.

HOURS
Lunch noon–2 P.M., dinner 6:30–11 P.M.

RESERVATIONS
No

CREDIT CARDS
MC, V

A LA CARTE
100F, BNC

PRIX FIXE
Lunch: 65F (buffet, *plat*, dessert) BC; dinner 90F, 3 courses, BNC

Au Buisson Ardent
25, rue Jussieu (5th)

This restaurant once sparked the beginning of a romance. The romance didn't last too long, but my affection for this old Left Bank landmark has never wavered. As most visitors to Paris soon learn, crowded dining tables are an accepted fact of French life. Here you will experience crowding at its height, especially at noon, when the place is positively jumping. Despite the hectic scene, you can enjoy a top-quality meal for a surprisingly reasonable tab. The truly fine bourgeoise cooking, prepared with sincerity and served in warm surroundings by pleasant middle-aged waitresses, has kept the well-fed regulars coming back for years.

First-class choices on the menu include a *salade de chèvre chaud*, leek *tarte, moules farcies, confit de canard maison, ris de veau*, leg of lamb, and any one of the fresh fish selections. All dishes are liberally garnished with two vegetables and some of the creamiest potatoes imaginable. Topping the dessert selections is the fruit *clafoutis*, or, in season, the *charlotte à la framboise*. The portions are dauntingly large, so arrive hungry!

TELEPHONE
43-54-93-02

MÉTRO
Jussieu

OPEN
Mon–Fri lunch and dinner

CLOSED
Sat, Sun; holidays; Aug

HOURS
Lunch noon–2:30 P.M., dinner 7:15–10 P.M.

RESERVATIONS
Yes

CREDIT CARDS
MC, V

A LA CARTE
130F, BNC

PRIX FIXE
Lunch: 70F, 3 courses, BNC; lunch and dinner: 120F, 4 courses, BC

Brasserie Balzar
49, rue des Écoles (5th)

TELEPHONE
43-54-13-67
MÉTRO
Odéon or Cluny
OPEN
Daily
CLOSED
Aug
HOURS
8 A.M.–1 A.M.,
continuous service
RESERVATIONS
Necessary
CREDIT CARDS
AE, DC, MC, V
A LA CARTE
150–180F, BNC
PRIX FIXE
None

You will find sawdust on the floor and graying waiters in white shirts and black cutaway vests in this genuine old brasserie, which was founded in 1890 by the same family who began Brasserie Lipp. Located close to the Sorbonne's sprawling campus, it has long been a favorite of Left Bank intellectuals and would-be bohemians of all types. Sartre and Camus were customers, and it is said that they had their last argument here. During the day you will find it has a faded charm, but one you will quickly learn to appreciate and enjoy as a reflection of the literary and political life of the *quartier*. In the evening the pace picks up, and the clientele is a bright mix of pipe-smoking professors, artists, actors, and pretty young women, making this one of the liveliest places in the Latin Quarter. Order the *steak au poivre* or the succulent *poulet rôti* (roast chicken), a basket of *pommes frites*, and a bottle of the house Beaujolais, and top it off with a piece of warm *tarte Tatin* for a good meal that will not strain your pocketbook.

Jardin des Pâtes
4, rue Lacépède (5th)

TELEPHONE
43-31-50-71
MÉTRO
Monge
OPEN
Tues–Sun lunch and dinner
CLOSED
Mon; 15 days in Jan;
last 2 weeks of Aug
HOURS
Lunch noon–2:30 P.M.,
dinner 7–10:30 P.M.
RESERVATIONS
No
CREDIT CARDS
V

Flowers and plants crowding the inside window, white walls hung with changing art exhibitions, and floating ceiling mobiles set the arty tone for this little *Cheap Eats* gem in the 5th where the food is definitely worth the hike from the nearest Métro.

Fresh food, simply served, is your guarantee from Mireille and Charles Maggio. Their specialty is imaginatively sauced pasta, made in-house from rice, corn, wheat, and rye flours ground daily in their own kitchen. Everything is a la carte and made to order, so the wait may seem a bit long, but once you taste their food, you will know you are on to something special. One of the most popular dishes is the *pâtes de chatigne*, a rich mix of pasta with duck fillet, mushrooms, *crème fraîche*, and just a hint of nutmeg. Another is the rice pasta topped with sautéed vegetables and chunks of tofu, and seasoned with fresh ginger. Rounding out the menu are soups, seasonal salads, and some rather heavy desserts considering the main courses. Worth serious consideration for all chocoholics, however, is the calories-don't-count chocolate-marmalade *tarte*.

A LA CARTE
85–100F, BNC
PRIX FIXE
None

La Fontaine Saint-Victor
Maison de la Mutualité, 24, rue St-Victor, off rue des Écoles (5th)

Who would ever want to eat here? I thought, as I arrived at the unimpressive French Social Security building just off Rue des Écoles. Things began to pick up as I walked up the expansive Art Deco staircase to the second-floor dining room. As I finished the last bite of my chocolate *profiteroles*, I knew why this *Cheap Eats* sleeper is so popular with the dignified French pensioners who have been lunching here for half a century.

From the bar you can order a gin and tonic or a dry martini for under 20F, a price barely changed since the restaurant opened. The service by white-jacketed waiters is flawless, the tables are set with linens and fresh flowers, the traditional menu is somewhat varied, the food is good, and above all, it is a bargain, whether you stick to the set menu or go a la carte. If you are in the neighborhood and looking for a quiet and proper lunch surrounded by sweet *grand'mères* and *grand-pères*, here is your restaurant.

TELEPHONE
40-46-12-04
MÉTRO
Cardinal-Lemoine, Maubert-Mutualité
OPEN
Daily, lunch only
CLOSED
Dinner; holidays; Aug
HOURS
Lunch 11:45 A.M.–2:30 P.M.
RESERVATIONS
Accepted for large groups only
CREDIT CARDS
V
A LA CARTE
88F, 4 courses, BNC
PRIX FIXE
100F, BNC

La Petite Légume
36, rue des Boulangers (5th)

"Live well, eat sensibly" is the motto at La Petite Légume. And you will, because a meal here is prepared without sugar, salt, or meat products and is served in a smoke-free atmosphere. For cash-strapped vegetarians or anyone else eager to jump onto the green bandwagon, this is a Cheap Eat worth noting. For less than 50F you can walk out guilt free and full of food that is good for you. The menu, in both English and French, lists something for every level of

TELEPHONE
40-46-06-85
MÉTRO
Cardinal Lemoine, Jussieu
OPEN
Mon–Fri shop, lunch, and dinner
CLOSED
Sat, Sun; holidays; Aug

HOURS
Shop 9:30 A.M.–10 P.M.,
restaurant lunch noon–
2:30 P.M., dinner 7–9:30 P.M.

RESERVATIONS
No

CREDIT CARDS
MC, V

A LA CARTE
40–70F, BC

PRIX FIXE
None

vegetarianism from whole-cereal dishes with seaweed, miso, and tofu to salads, soups, and the overflowing plat du jour of *crudités*, rice or grains, vegetables, dried fruit, and nuts. Order a nonalcoholic beer or a tumbler of carrot juice and indulge in a slice of their nonfat cheesecake or chocolate cake to round out the repast. Don't have time to stop for a meal? They will pack everything to go and even charge a bit less to do so. On your way out, take a minute or two to glance through the shop, which sells macrobiotic books and natural products.

La Rôtisserie du Beaujolais
19, quai de la Tournelle (5th)

TELEPHONE
43-54-17-47

MÉTRO
Maubert-Mutualité or Pont-
Marie

OPEN
Tues–Sun lunch and dinner

CLOSED
Mon; major holidays; NAC

HOURS
Lunch noon–2:30 P.M., dinner
7:30–11:30 P.M.

RESERVATIONS
Essential

CREDIT CARDS
MC, V

A LA CARTE
170F, BNC

PRIX FIXE
None

Almost every international gourmet has made a pilgrimage to Claude Terrail's La Tour d'Argent, with its glorious view of Notre-Dame Cathedral, its high prices, and its famous pressed duck. Recognizing the growing demand for a return to the old-fashioned basics of French food, Claude Terrail opened La Rôtisserie du Beaujolais a few steps away on the Rue de la Tournelle. Here faithful Parisian patrons sit elbow to elbow along rows of banquettes in two rooms with an open kitchen, or at tables on a glassed-in terrace overlooking the Seine. They feast on the finest food prepared from the freshest ingredients from Lyon. The best sausages and *chèvre* cheeses from this gourmet mecca are eaten with *pain gris*, or gray bread, baked next door at La Tour d'Argent. Succulent leg of lamb, quail, chicken, and squab are roasted to perfection before the customers' eyes on a traditional roasting spit and served with tender *pommes frites*. Waiters dish up salads and desserts from a serving table in the main room, and chefs decked out in checked pants and long aprons relax at the Art Deco zinc bar between cooking rounds at the large roasting oven. The only kind of wine served is Beaujolais, poured out of hand-painted glass carafes into thick old bistro glasses.

L'Assiette aux Fromages
27, rue Mouffetard

Smile, say "cheese," and head for L'Assiette aux Fromages. France is reported to produce over 400 varieties of cheese, a fact that can be overwhelming to anyone used to only Roquefort, Cheddar, and Swiss. Now cheese-lovers of all types can taste, eat, and buy more than 199 varieties of cheese from all over France in this bright, modern *fromagerie* with its garden restaurant, not far from Place de la Contrescarpe on the colorful Rue Mouffetard.

The menu, which is beautifully explained in English and German as well as French, offers many enticing cheese-inspired dishes, from salads and sandwiches to quiches, *tartes*, *raclettes*, fondues, and good desserts. The smart move here, however, is to order one of the *plateaux des fromages*, which have five regional or specialty cheeses per plate: *doucer* (mild), *saveur* (strong), *chèvre* (goat), *l'avergnat* (cheese from the Auvergne), *suspens* (their selection), and *personnalisé* (five cheeses of your choice from a list of eleven). All cheese plates are served with pots of sweet butter, crusty baguettes, and *pain Poilâne*. It is great to go for lunch with a small group, order several different plates of cheese, have a couple of bottles of the house red wine, and then walk off the consequences in the nearby Jardin des Plantes.

TELEPHONE
45-35-14-21

MÉTRO
Monge

OPEN
Thurs–Tues shop and restaurant

CLOSED
Wed; Feb 5–Mar 15

HOURS
Cheese shop 9:30 A.M.–10 P.M., restaurant noon–11 P.M.; continuous service

RESERVATIONS
No

CREDIT CARDS
MC, V

A LA CARTE
70–110F, BNC

PRIX FIXE
None

Le Baptiste
11, rue des Boulangers (5th)

You can eat, drink, and be merry at Le Baptiste without it costing you an arm and a leg. The service is friendly, the crowd good-natured, and you are bound to have a good time sitting at one of the long trestle tables and stuffing yourself along with the students and locals who have made this budget-priced spot so popular for smart Cheap Eaters. Located in an ancient building on a narrow 700-year-old cobblestone street, this rustic restaurant has enough wooden beams and stone to build a real farm. The inside is

TELEPHONE
43-25-57-24

MÉTRO
Jussieu

OPEN
Mon–Fri lunch and dinner, Sat dinner only

CLOSED
Sat lunch, Sun; 1 week at Christmas; NAC

HOURS
Lunch noon–2 P.M., dinner 7–10:30 P.M.

lighted by antique brass-and-ceramic lamps, and the stone walls are hung with changing exhibits of local artists' paintings and drawings.

Sturdy *terrines* and sizable salads will whet your appetite for the main courses of beef, duck, fish, lamb, or one of the daily plats du jour, followed by what the menu accurately describes as an "avalanche of desserts."

Le Berthoud
1, rue Valette (5th)

TELEPHONE
43-54-38-81
MÉTRO
Maubert-Mutualité
OPEN
Mon–Fri lunch and dinner,
Sat dinner only
CLOSED
Sat lunch, Sun; holidays; July
and Aug
HOURS
Lunch noon–2:30 P.M.,
dinner 7:30 P.M.–1 A.M.
RESERVATIONS
Advised for dinner
CREDIT CARDS
V
A LA CARTE
190F, BNC
PRIX FIXE
None

A friendly welcome, comfortable seating, tapestry-hung walls, and a stunning collection of hand-painted glass lamps with beaded fringe shades create the atmosphere for unusual dining at Le Berthoud. Plan to ignore your diet, forget your cholesterol count, and sit back and enjoy the sumptuous natural cuisine of the multitalented owner-chef, Mme Suzanne Knych, who has been cooking in this charming restaurant for 32 years. Her creative touch with food makes dining here not just another meal, but a culinary event. All recipes are Mme Knych's own, and she uses only fresh ingredients free from artificial coloring, chemicals, or flavor enhancers. You will taste the delicious difference in her freshly made butter, *terrines*, soups, sauces, cheeses, and desserts.

The vegetable *mousselines* are meals in themselves, and you owe it to yourself to try the Vivaldi: a mélange of spinach, carrots, cauliflower, and leeks dressed in a light cheese sauce. During the warmer months, a special light menu is available offering cold soups, beautiful vegetable-based salads, and cold meat plates. The heavenly desserts are Mme Knych's own artistically presented pastries, cakes, and ice creams, with such fanciful names as *cuisse de mademoiselle*, Damnation, Iceberg, *exquis*, and *bellissimo*. In addition to her wide-ranging cooking skills, Mme Knych is an internationally acclaimed artist and the author of several natural foods cookbooks. While you might not be able to take one of her paintings home, you

RESERVATIONS
No
CREDIT CARDS
MC, V
A LA CARTE
90–110F, BNC
PRIX FIXE

can buy one of her cookbooks (in French only) so you can re-create her magic in your own kitchen.

Le Bistro d'Hannah
9, rue de Pontoise (5th)

Since its opening barely two years ago, this bistro near Notre-Dame has become an address dear to the hearts of lovers of Beaujolais and Bordeaux wines and Angus beef. It is named after the owner's daughter, who was born just after the restaurant opened. You can see her picture hanging above the entry door.

Owner Eric Narcyz changes the wine selections monthly, and many can be ordered by the glass or the half bottle. Angus beef, specially flown in from northern Scotland, forms the mainstay of the menu. However, if you are not a red-meat eater, there are plenty of other delicious selections to tempt you, such as *confit de poule, canard, lapin,* or a spicy grilled *andouillette*. After the heavy meal, the coffee parfait with Kahlúa is a refreshing ending.

TELEPHONE
43-54-68-23
MÉTRO
Maubert-Mutualité
OPEN
Wed–Sun lunch and dinner
CLOSED
Mon–Tues; major holidays; Aug
HOURS
Lunch noon–2:30 P.M., dinner 7:30–10:30 P.M.
RESERVATIONS
Advised
CREDIT CARDS
AE, DC, MC, V
A LA CARTE
125–140F, BNC
PRIX FIXE
Lunch: 79F, *entrée, plat,* and coffee or *plat,* dessert, coffee (wine not included); dinner: 139F, 3 courses, 2 glasses of wine

Le Grenier de Notre-Dame
18, rue de la Bûcherie (5th)

It's a natural—and besides, it is good, not too expensive, and smoke free. In the past, hard-pressed vegetarians have had to settle for some rather beige, boring, and bland excuses for "health food" in Paris. But no more. At this two-tiered garden restaurant in the shadow of Notre-Dame, even confirmed carnivores are regulars.

The long menu lists tasty soups, copious salads, omelettes of every variety, fresh-squeezed juices, homemade pastas, jazz main courses, natural cheeses, great desserts, and even organic wines. Each table has its own bottle of extra-virgin olive oil, soy sauce, *gomazio* (ground sesame seeds and sea salt), and a bottle of Levure de Bière, a malt substance to drizzle over soups or salads.

The student-backed service can sometimes fall into the rude and "care-less" category, but this is still

TELEPHONE
43-29-98-29
MÉTRO
Maubert-Mutualité
OPEN
Wed–Mon lunch and dinner
CLOSED
Tues (winter months); Aug closing varies
HOURS
Lunch noon–2:30 P.M., dinner 7–11 P.M.
RESERVATIONS
No
CREDIT CARDS
AE, DC, MC, V
A LA CARTE
75–110F, BNC
PRIX FIXE
75F, 3 courses, BNC

one of the best vegetarian restaurants in Paris, with something for everyone, from hardcore macrobiotics and habitual health nuts, to dedicated dieters and anyone else in search of a wholesome meal in pretty surroundings.

Le Mouffetard
116, rue Mouffetard, corner of rue des Postes (5th)

TELEPHONE
43-31-42-50
MÉTRO
Censier-Daubenton
OPEN
Tues–Sun
CLOSED
Mon; July; 10 days at Christmas
HOURS
Tues–Sat 7 A.M.–9 P.M., Sunday 7 A.M.–4 P.M.; continuous service
RESERVATIONS
No
CREDIT CARDS
None
A LA CARTE
80F, BNC
PRIX FIXE
None

In the 15th century, Rue Mouffetard was known as Hell Raisers' Hill because of the many taverns and brothels in the area. The steep street that begins at the Place de la Contrescarp and winds down to the St-Mediard Church near the Censier-Daubenton Métro stop is still full of greasy spoons and probably a brothel or two if you look hard enough. The best reason to go there today is to wander through the colorful open-air morning *marché* and the many inexpensive clothing and shoe shops that line both sides of the long street. When you go, be sure to stop in at a little down-to-earth-spot known as Café Mouffetard, Caves Mouffetard, Le Mouffetard, or Brasserie Mouffetard, depending on whether you read the name of the building, the menu, the business card, or the check.

The café has been owned and run by the members of the Chartran family for years, and they get up with the chickens to serve locals on their way to work. Arrive a little later in the morning and you can indulge in the house specialties: buttery croissants and rich yeasty brioches made every day by M. and Mme Chartran. At lunchtime, try the rabbit in a tangy mustard sauce or the thickly sliced ham with braised endives for a typical workingman's lunch. Even if you are not up to sharing an eye-opening Cognac with the locals at dawn, you should go before noon to capture the feeling of a street market at its best.

Le Raccard
19, rue Laplace (5th)

TELEPHONE
43-54-83-75, 43-25-27-27

With a group or just one other person, Le Raccard

is the place to fill up on the lip-smacking Swiss specialties of fondue and *raclette*. *Raclette*, for the uninitiated, is bubbling hot melted cheese served over boiled new potatoes and accompanied with tangy *cornichons* and pickled onions—and it is as delectable as it is filling and fattening.

The Swiss-style chalet is located not far from the Panthéon and is worth the short climb from the Métro because you definitely need a good appetite when eating here. Stay with the house specialties and you won't go away unhappy. The desserts, which you won't have room for anyway, are best forgotten. The waiters can be impatient, but when pushed, do speak enough English to suggest appropriate combinations. Before leaving, be sure to notice the authentic hay crib, or *raccard*, in the back, which has been skillfully turned into a little bar.

MÉTRO
Maubert-Mutualité

OPEN
Tues–Sun dinner only

CLOSED
Mon; lunch; 15 days in Aug

HOURS
Dinner 7:30 P.M.–12:30 A.M.

RESERVATIONS
Advised on weekends in winter

CREDIT CARDS
AE, DC, MC, V

A LA CARTE
150F, BNC

PRIX FIXE
None

Le Vieux Chêne
69, rue Mouffetard (5th)

The Rue Mouffetard is lined with restaurants, most of which reach out for tourist wallets and credit cards with loud music, gaudy fake decor, windows full of sizzling meats, and sweaty chefs preparing poor fare. This one, where all the locals go, is different: it serves wonderful food that fits into almost any budget, and it is charming. Owner Francis Tartare has been serving his guests for almost 10 years. At lunch you can usually find him seated with friends at the table by the front window. Every day he sets 35 places for lunch and dinner on paper-covered tables. In the evening, linen napkins and brass hurricane lamps add a touch of formality. The chef changes the very short menu at least once a week and uses seasonal ingredients in preparing the traditional French cuisine. Some favorites you can hope to taste include the *gratin de moules et poireaux* (mussels and leeks in a light sauce, topped with a cheesy crust); sausage and lentils; lamb with an unusual asparagus sauce, and a cinnamon-apple tart. Three different reasonably priced wines are featured each week.

TELEPHONE
43-37-71-51

MÉTRO
Monge

OPEN
Tues–Sat lunch and dinner

CLOSED
Sun and Mon; holidays; NAC

HOURS
Lunch noon–2 P.M., dinner
8 P.M.–midnight

RESERVATIONS
Advised

CREDIT CARDS
None

A LA CARTE
160F, BNC

PRIX FIXE
Lunch: 65F, 3 courses, BNC;
lunch and dinner, 120F,
3 courses, BNC

Moissonnier
28, rue des Fossés St-Bernard (5th)

TELEPHONE
43-29-87-65
MÉTRO
Cardinal-Lemoine
OPEN
Tues–Sat lunch and dinner;
Sun lunch only
CLOSED
Sun dinner, Mon; Aug
HOURS
Lunch noon–2 P.M.,
dinner 7–10 P.M.
RESERVATIONS
Necessary
CREDIT CARDS
V
A LA CARTE
220F, BNC
PRIX FIXE
None

The pleasure of dining at Moissonnier has not faded with time, as it continues to be a perfect example of a fine French family-owned bistro. As he has for almost 35 years, Louis Moissonnier prepares hearty Lyonnaise dishes; his attractive wife Jannine receives the top-drawer clientele, which includes French president François Mitterand. The best seating in the two-floor restaurant is on the ground floor, with its high ceiling, massive bouquet of fresh flowers, and tiny service bar along one side.

The well-rounded selection of native dishes makes this an excellent dining choice; it is also a true culinary value considering the high quality of the food, which is prepared from scratch on the premises every day. "Our menu never changes," says M. Moissonnier. "Our clients come here when they are feeling nostalgic for the kind of food they ate when they were children." A good *entrée* choice is the *saladier*, a large cart rolled to your table laden with salads, *terrines*, herring in cream, marinated vegetables, and many other tempting appetizers. This is followed by the main course, which could be fillets of sole on a bed of fresh spinach, or an outstanding rack of lamb with potatoes au gratin. Complete the meal with an assortment of fine regional cheeses, a light meringue filled with ice cream and surrounded by hot chocolate, or a seasonally perfect *tartlette aux fraises.*

Perraudin
157, rue St-Jacques (5th)

TELEPHONE
46-33-15-75
MÉTRO
Luxembourg
OPEN
Tues–Fri lunch and dinner,
Sat and Mon dinner only
CLOSED
Mon and Sat lunch, Sun; NAC

For decades, Perraudin has demonstrated the glory of substantial French cooking. Possessing a winning combination for Cheap Eaters, it has un-fussy food, good wine, an authentic atmosphere, and realistic prices. In addition, children are welcome. Sitting at one of the little bistro tables, looking at the classic menu and the cast of faithfuls sitting around the room, you will soon have the feeling that nothing has changed here for years—and you will be right.

After polishing off weighty servings of smoked herring with warm potato salad or tangy onion *tartes*, well-fed diners tuck into main courses of roast veal with noodles, poached salmon, grilled steaks, and popular daily specials. Wine can be anything from a glass or pitcher of the house variety to a little-known regional *cru* seldom seen in Paris. Owner Hubert Gloaguen (who also owns Le Bistro d'André, page 132), and his sister, Marie-Christine Kvella, who manages Perraudin, are justly proud of their wine *cave* and its wide-ranging, undiscovered selections.

HOURS
Lunch noon–2:30 P.M., dinner 7:30–10 P.M.

RESERVATIONS
No

CREDIT CARDS
None

A LA CARTE
Lunch only: 59F, 3 courses, BNC

PRIX FIXE
100F, BNC

Restaurant Chez Marius
30, rue des Fossés-Saint-Bernard (5th)

When an enthusiastic reader wrote to me about Chez Marius, saying he had eaten there every night for a week and had even had a button sewn on his coat by the proprietor Mme Pourchers, I knew this was one I had to try. I did and I am happy to report that it is every bit as wonderful as it was described. The homey and comfortable interior looks as though it hasn't changed much in years, and most of the robust dining regulars settle in at their favorite table as though they were dining in their own kitchen. The best seating is definitely downstairs, with its beautifully tiled floor, mirrored bar, and tables dressed white linen and a bouquet of fresh flowers.

When ordering, plan to stay with the lower-priced prix fixe menu, which includes wine, or the price of the meal could quickly get out of hand. This menu offers ample choices and changes every two or three weeks, but it always includes the meltingly tender beef tournedos and the *côte de veau grand'mère*. The desserts are limited in number, but are all *maison* and good, especially the fresh fruit *tarte*, one of their specialties.

TELEPHONE
43-54-19-01

MÉTRO
Cardinal-Lemoine

OPEN
Sun–Tues, Thurs–Fri lunch and dinner; Sat dinner only

CLOSED
Wed; Sat lunch, major holidays; NAC

HOURS
Lunch 12:15–2 P.M., dinner 7:30 –10:30 P.M.

RESERVATIONS
Advised

CREDIT CARDS
AE, DC, MC, V

A LA CARTE
200F, BNC

PRIX FIXE
120F, 3 courses, BC; 170F, 4 courses, BNC

SIXTH ARRONDISSEMENT

SIXTH ARRONDISSEMENT
Left Bank: École des Beaux-Arts, Luxembourg Gardens, Odéon National Theater, Place St-Michel, St-Germain-des-Prés Church (the oldest in Paris), St-Sulpice (murals by Delacroix)

The sixth is a continuation of the Latin Quarter, but *plus chic.* The emphasis is on art galleries, antiques, and expensive restaurants and boutiques. Two famous cafés are here: Café des Deux Magots and Café de Flore. These spots, which offer some of the best people-watching in the city, were the prime haunts of the existentialists of the postwar years.

SIXTH ARRONDISSEMENT RESTAURANTS

À la Cour de Rohan
Au Petit Prince
Aux Charpentiers
Chez Claude Sainlouis
Chez Maître Paul
Chez Wadja
Crémerie-Restaurant
  Polidor
Guenmaï
La Chocolatière
La Lozère
La Marlotte
L'Attrape Coeur

L'Écaille de P.C.B.
Le Caméléon
L'Écluse
Le Petit Saint-Benoît
Le Petit Vatel
L'Heure Gourmande
Mariage Frères
Restaurant des Arts
Restaurant des Beaux
  Arts
San Francisco Muffin
  Company

À la Cour de Rohan
59–61, rue St-André-des-Arts; enter through Cour du Commerce St-André (6th)

TELEPHONE
43-25-79-67
MÉTRO
St-Michel, Odéon
OPEN
Tues–Sun
CLOSED
Mon; Aug
HOURS
Tues–Fri and Sun noon–7:30 P.M. (later hours in summer), Sat noon–11:30 P.M.; continuous service

Situated in an 18th-century *passage* that runs between Boulevard St-Germain and Rue St-André-des-Arts, À la Cour de Rohan has become a Left Bank fixture as a place to go with a friend for an intimate afternoon of gossip or romance, or to listen to slow jazz on a quiet Saturday night. The downstairs room overlooking the *passage* is crowded with tables and a big hutch displaying high-calorie temptations. I prefer to sit upstairs, where the frilly chintz curtains, well-worn English furniture, and aromas of tea remind me of a maiden auntie's British parlor.

Lobster bisque, quiches, salads, creamy hot dishes,

fined and comfortable. The nicely spaced tables are formally set with starched linens, fresh flowers, and sparkling crystal in a soft gray room with subdued lighting and good artwork on the walls.

The country-style cuisine continues to feature specialties from the Franche-Comté region in eastern France. Among the *entrées* you will find a *terrine maison*, a plate of garlicky sausages served warm with tiny potatoes, and, in season, fat white asparagus in a warm vinaigrette. A main-course must is the *poulet au vin jaune*: tender chicken in a tomato, mushroom, and wine sauce. Most of the other main dishes are also served with Jura wine sauces that are perfect for mopping up with crusty baguettes. If you can still think about dessert, the *crème brûlée* is definitely worthwhile, and the local cheeses are interesting.

CLOSED
Sat lunch, Sun, Mon; major holidays; Aug

HOURS
Lunch noon–2:30 P.M., dinner 7–10:30 P.M.

RESERVATIONS
Definitely

CREDIT CARDS
AE, DC, MC, V

A LA CARTE
185F, BNC

PRIX FIXE
165F, 3 courses, BC

Chez Wadja
10, rue de la Grande-Chaumière (6th)

Since the 1930s, Chez Wadja has been dear to the hearts of dedicated budgeters as an old-fashioned cheapie serving belt-popping portions of home cooking. The menu is handwritten daily on tablet paper and clipped to the sagging front-window curtain. Seating is around oilcloth-covered tables in a room boasting about as much atmosphere as a bus station. If you do eat here, you *must* keep in mind where you are and keep your gourmet expectations to a minimum.

Show up early, take a seat, and roll up your sleeves for Marie Kowalezyk's daily specials of goulash, ravioli, *blanquette de veau*, *hachis Parmentier* (ground beef with mashed potatoes), pork roast, and *chou farci*, (stuffed cabbage). She cooks everything herself in an old kitchen in the back, and the dishes are served by her two brothers Léon and Casimir, who have worked here since World War II—pictures of the brothers with American G.I.'s are on the wall to prove it. As you can imagine, Mme Kowalezyk and her brothers are not kids anymore, and retirement is just around the cor-

TELEPHONE
43-25-66-90

MÉTRO
Vavin

OPEN
Mon–Sat lunch and dinner

CLOSED
Sun; holidays; Aug

HOURS
Lunch noon–2:30 P.M., dinner 7–9:30 P.M.

RESERVATIONS
No

CREDIT CARDS
None

A LA CARTE
55F, BNC

PRIX FIXE
50F, BNC

ner—so visit this Parisian family restaurant before they hang the permanent CLOSED sign on the door.

Crémerie-Restaurant Polidor
41, rue Monsieur-le-Prince (6th)

TELEPHONE
43-26-95-34

MÉTRO
Odéon

OPEN
Daily lunch and dinner

CLOSED
Dec 24 and 25; NAC

HOURS
Lunch noon–2:30 P.M.,
Mon–Sat dinner 7 P.M.–1 A.M.,
Sun dinner 7–11 P.M.

RESERVATIONS
No

CREDIT CARDS
None

A LA CARTE
90F, BNC

PRIX FIXE
Mon–Fri lunch: 50F,
3 courses, BNC

With its well-worn tile floor, long lines of tables, and huge wall mirrors reflecting polished brass hat racks, old Paris posters, and pretty Belle Époque lights, this relic of a bygone era is now a bit touristy, but still loved by almost everyone. The entire restaurant, including the courtyard toilet, has been declared a historical monument. Among other holdovers from the past still in use are rows of numbered post office–like boxes along the back wall, which contain the silver-ringed cloth napkins of the regular customers. Founded in 1845, the restaurant is listed in virtually every guidebook, and everything said about it is true, from the solid, inexpensive food to the fact that it has been the haunt of such literary figures as André Gide, Ernest Hemingway, James Joyce, Jack Kerouac, and a host of others.

The food is served quickly by squads of rushing waitresses to students, workers in undershirts, pensioners wearing berets, and more than a few tourists. A daily menu (translated into English) offers such comforting standbys as *boeuf bourguignon, lapin à la moutarde,* guinea hen with curly cabbage, *boudin noir* (blood sausage), and sensational fresh fruit *tartes.*

Guenmaï
6, rue Cardinale (6th)

TELEPHONE
43-26-03-24

MÉTRO
St-Gérmain-des-Pres

OPEN
Mon–Sat shop and restaurant

CLOSED
Sun; holidays; Aug

HOURS
Shop 9 A.M.–8:30 P.M.,
restaurant 11:45 A.M.–3:30 P.M.

What are all these people doing milling around the steps of this natural foods restaurant/shop with plates of food in their hands? I wondered as I strolled by. When I could get close enough to look in, I could see others sitting on tiny stools balancing plates on their knees, and still more would-be-diners standing ten-deep waiting to get into the tiny dining room. I knew that Guenmaï had to be offering something very good to attract such a crowd in a neighborhood the patron's wife, Mme Faucher. Another sure sign of quality is the mixed crowd: businesspeople next to a table of rosy-cheeked elderly couples next to a young couple busy falling in love. The are all sitting elbow-to-elbow along banquettes or at marble-topped tables in the center of the room and digging into steaming plates of hearty bistro fare with a real personality.

The menu changes two or three times a year, but you can always count on having *courgettes marinées au citron* (raw grated zucchini in a lemon marinade), *mousse d'aubergines au saumon* (eggplant mousse surrounded by slices of smoked salmon), and the superb *salade de haricots verts et foie gras* (pencil-slim green beans in a garlicky vinaigrette, topped with satiny foie gras. For the main course, the veal with noodles, *confit de canard* (preserved duck), and braised beef with carrots keep the regulars coming back time and again. For dessert, you absolutely *must* try the *fondant au poires*, a pear cake made from an old recipe of the patron's grandmother. When it is served, you will think it is too big a slice to finish. Let me assure you, you will eat every crumb and wish for more.

There is just one thing you must never do at Le Caméléon, and that is forget to reserve at least a day or two in advance for both lunch and dinner.

CLOSED
Sun, Mon; holidays; Aug

HOURS
Lunch noon–2 P.M.,
dinner 8–11 P.M.

RESERVATIONS
Essential

CREDIT CARDS
None

A LA CARTE
180F, BNC

PRIX FIXE
None

L'Écluse (Grands-Augustins)
15, quai de Grands-Augustins (6th)
Telephone: 46-33-58-74
Métro: St-Michel
See page 42.

Le Petit Saint-Benoît
4, rue St-Benoît (6th)

This is a marvelous bistro smack in the heart of St-Germain-des-Près. The interior is vintage Paris: brown walls, brass hat racks, fresh white paper covering red-checked tablecloths, and a big, lazy dog crowding the busiest aisle. Outside several hotly fought-over sidewalk tables offer ringside seating for the passing parade. Motherly waitresses serve a cross-

TELEPHONE
42-60-27-92

MÉTRO
St-Germain-des-Près

OPEN
Mon–Fri lunch and dinner

CLOSED
Sat, Sun; holidays; NAC

HOURS
Lunch noon–2:30 P.M.,
dinner 7–10 P.M.
RESERVATIONS
No
CREDIT CARDS
None
A LA CARTE
85F, BNC
PRIX FIXE
None

section of intellectuals, B.C.B.G.'s (*bon chic bon genre*: French yuppies), artists, and portly French men with young, stylishly-clad companions. The handwritten mimeographed menu lists low-priced basics that are cooked to a T and served in portions worthy of the seriously hungry. Start with a soothing vegetable soup and go on to a nourishing serving of braised beef with carrots, grilled lamb chops, or roast chicken. Top it all off with a pitcher of the house wine and a bowl of rice pudding. Lingering over a *café express*, you will no doubt begin to seriously consider moving to Paris.

Le Petit Vatel
5, rue Lobineau (6th)

TELEPHONE
43-54-28-49
MÉTRO
Mabillon
OPEN
Mon–Sat lunch and dinner,
Sun dinner only
CLOSED
Sun lunch; major holidays;
NAC
HOURS
Lunch noon–3 P.M.,
dinner 7–midnight
RESERVATIONS
No
CREDIT CARDS
V
A LA CARTE
60–85F, BNC
PRIX FIXE
Lunch only: 58F, large salad, 1
garnished *plat* or 1 *entrée* and
dessert; BNC

While not a place to impress your mother-in-law, Mary Bousquet's little Left Bank treasure is a good choice for the hardcore Cheap Eater who is young at heart. At Le Petit Vatel, you won't eat the most refined food in Paris, but you might have some of the most interesting company. Seated on hard stools or bentwood chairs around wooden tables, everyone eats together in a tiny room that used to be dominated by a large pink 1914 cookstove, with the chef presiding over the bubbling pots. Recently, the stove was judged to be a fire hazard and authorities forced Mary to remove it. In its place, she installed another table or two and a photo of the once-famous stove that provided Cheap Eats for so many for so long. Fortunately, the stove is the only thing missing; the Cheap Eats are still here and in abundance. The daily menu, written on a big blackboard, includes seasonal soups, salads, moussaka, pork with herbs, roast turkey, and vegetarian plates. For dessert there is a choice of homemade *fromage blanc*, chocolate cake, crème caramel, or a piece of cheese. Wine, beer, and cider are served in pitchers.

L'Heure Gourmande
22, passage Dauphine, between rue Mazarine and rue Dauphine (6th)

Every Parisian neighborhood has its share of tea-rooms, those gentle places that nourish the body and soothe the soul. A visit to L'Heure Gourmande, hidden in an obscure courtyard between Rue Mazarine and Rue Dauphine, will definitely nourish both body and soul, and provide a peaceful place to while away an hour or two over a quiet meal or a pot of tea and dessert.

Once you find it, you will be charmed by the open and airy interior, with its big picture windows overlooking a garden courtyard. I think it is best to sit downstairs near the ornate sideboard holding a fantasy of calorie-charged desserts, where you can admire the extensive collection of tea-and coffeepots displayed around the room.

The well-conceived cuisine features a wealth of interesting salads, egg dishes, an all-day brunch, and those oh, so tempting desserts. If you order a salad, you will have many succulent choices, including the *assiette vahine* (with stuffed veal, *taboulé*, and mixed greens) and the *assiette Petrouchka* (a bed of greens covered with smoked salmon, *tarama*, salmon eggs, creamed cucumbers, and blinis), all washed down with a shot or two of Russian vodka. Genteel service, air-conditioning, and a warm welcome from owner Mme Courtemanche make this delightful find even more appealing.

TELEPHONE
46-34-00-40

MÉTRO
Odéon

OPEN
Mon–Sat

CLOSED
Sun; dinner; May 1–8, Dec 24–Jan 3; 3 weeks in Aug; major holidays

HOURS
11 A.M.–7 P.M., continuous service; tea 2–7 P.M.

RESERVATIONS
Necessary for lunch

CREDIT CARDS
V

A LA CARTE
75–100F, BNC

PRIX FIXE
Brunch 120F, BC

Mariage Frères

13, rue des Grands-Augustins (6th)
Telephone: 40-51-82-50
Métro: St-Michel
Prix Fixe: Sat and Sun brunch: 150F, BC, 185F, BC

See page 69.

Restaurant des Arts

73, rue de Seine (6th)

Restaurant des Arts is around the corner from the picturesque Rue de Buci street *marché*. Surprisingly

TELEPHONE
None

MÉTRO
Mabillon
OPEN
Mon–Thurs lunch and dinner;
Fri lunch only
CLOSED
Fri dinner, Sat and Sun; Easter
week; 2 weeks at Christmas;
Aug
HOURS
Lunch noon–2:30 P.M.,
dinner 7–9:30 P.M.
RESERVATIONS
No
CREDIT CARDS
None
A LA CARTE
85–120F, BNC
PRIX FIXE
75F, 3 courses, BNC

undiscovered by the tourists that throng this part of Paris, the restaurant has been humming along since the twenties—quite a testimony to the consistent quality and low prices of the homespun food that has been served to *quartier* residents by two generations of the Manceau family.

A neatly typed *carte* changes daily and offers reassuring, familiar fare. Among the simple choices you will find such *entrée* favorites as *crudités, lentilles vinaigrette,* and *salade composé* (with rice, corn, tuna, and tomatoes). For the *plat,* a wide choice includes roast chicken, beef tongue—either cold or in a tomato sauce—and veal prepared several ways. The desserts will bring back fond memories of boarding school days with such long-forgotten jewels as rice pudding, custard, and apple compote with freshly ground nutmeg.

Restaurant des Beaux Arts
11, rue Bonaparte (6th)

TELEPHONE
43-26-92-64
MÉTRO
St-Germain-des-Prés
OPEN
Daily lunch and dinner
CLOSED
Christmas Day; NAC
HOURS
Lunch noon–2:30 P.M.,
dinner 7–11 P.M.
RESERVATIONS
No
CREDIT CARDS
None
A LA CARTE
85–100F, BNC
PRIX FIXE
68F, 3 courses, BC

If you want to know what student life was like in the past in Paris, eat at Restaurant des Beaux Arts, one of the most famous student stomping grounds, both then and now. The dining rooms are busy and cramped, but not enough to discourage the faithful. The best seating is on the main floor, where you get a full view of the bubbling pots in the kitchen, the beautiful bar, the baskets of fresh baguettes, and the murals painted by students from l'École Nationale des Beaux-Arts, just across the street. Upstairs, the mood is more relaxed, but definitely not as much fun. Although not quite the cheap thrill it once was, the menu is long and plentiful and is definitely a bargain considering the size of the portions. All the standards are here, from *oeuf dur mayonnaise* (hard-boiled egg and mayonnaise), grilled sardines, and *crudités* (mixed raw vegetables), to *boeuf bourguignon,* grilled chicken, mountains of *frites* (fries), fruit tarts, and crème caramel. With a pitcher of the house wine or a mug of beer, you will probably get away with spending less than 80F for a filling lunch or dinner.

San Francisco Muffin Company

35, rue du Dragon (6th)
Telephone: 45-48-45-55
Métro: St-Germain-des-Prés
Open: Mon–Sat
Closed: Sun; major holidays; Aug

See page 70.

SEVENTH ARRONDISSEMENT

SEVENTH ARRONDISSEMENT
Left Bank: Champ-de-Mars,
École Militaire, Eiffel Tower,
Invalides (the final resting place
for Napoléon), Musée d'Orsay,
National Assembly, Rodin
Museum, UNESCO

The right Paris zip code is 007 and has been since the early 1700s when blue-blooded families fled Versailles and settled in this part of Paris. A sense of good living and a feeling of luxury pervade the streets of this *beau-quartier*, where fashionable people live and pay high rents, and young chic meets old guard. The handsome tree-shaded avenues are lined with government offices, foreign embassies, beautiful shops, intimate hotels, and outstanding restaurants.

The seventh is also the most food-conscious, with some of the best bakers, *charcuteries, traiteurs*, cheese and pastry shops, and confectioners to be found in the city.

SEVENTH ARRONDISSEMENT RESTAURANTS

Aux Petits Oignons	Le Mâconnais
Bar de la Maison de	Le Petit Niçois
l'Amérique Latine	Le Petit Tronquet
Chez l'Ami Jean	Le Relais Saint-Germain
La Fontaine de Mars	Le Sancerre
La Pie Gourmande	L'Oeillade
La Poule au Pot	L'Olympic
L'Auberge Bressane	Restaurant Chez
L'Auvergne	Germaine
Gourmande	Restaurant du Palais
Le Bistrot de Breteuil	d'Orsay

Aux Petits Oignons
29, rue de Bellechasse (7th)

TELEPHONE
47-05-48-77
MÉTRO
Solférino
OPEN
Mon–Sat lunch and dinner
CLOSED
Sun; holidays; Aug
HOURS
Lunch noon–2 P.M.,
dinner 8–11 P.M.

Good manners and gentility are as much at home here as the local regulars who have made this bistro a neighborhood fixture. They all vie for one of the nine tables in the downstairs dining room, which is simply decorated with tiny floral prints draped over white tablecloths and accented by maroon napkins. Reliable everyday cooking at moderate prices is served without fireworks or blunders. There is a prix fixe lunch menu, and an à la carte menu for both lunch and dinner. Aux Petits Oignons is known for its *magret de canard à la confiture de petits oignons* (duck breast with onion jam) and *foie de veau aux avocats* (veal liver with avocados). A word of advice: leave room for the famed chocolate cake with a shaved chocolate topping, or the *goûter de tantine* (a pudding with apples, candied fruits, and caramel sauce on top).

RESERVATIONS
Advised for dinner

CREDIT CARDS
MC, V

A LA CARTE
130–140F, BNC

PRIX FIXE
Lunch only: 94F, 3 courses, BNC

Bar de la Maison de l'Amérique Latine
217, boulevard St-Germain (7th)

No matter how wonderful French food is, sometimes a taste of the food we love to eat at home hits the spot. If you are a Mexican foodie and have such an attack, head straight for the Bar de la Maison de l'Amérique Latine. This cultural center occupies an *hôtel particulier* built by Jacques Gabriel in 1704. The restaurant serves formal French food in formal surroundings at *very* formal prices. The food served in the relaxed bar is another matter. It is all South of the Border fare and mighty good indeed—and so are the prices in comparison to other Mexican restaurants in Paris. All your favorites are here: guacamole, tostadas, *carne asada*, and the daily specials Mexican-food-lovers have come to count on. Monday is reserved for quesadillas, Tuesday for chili, and on Wednesday it is chicken enchiladas. *Feijoada* (the national dish of Brazil) is the Thursday treat, and *sancocho de pescado* (fish) is served on Friday. Tired of French wines? Then order a piña colada, a Margarita cooler, or a bottle of Mexican wine or beer to accompany your repast.

TELEPHONE
45-49-33-23

MÉTRO
Rue du Bac

OPEN
Mon–Fri lunch and dinner

CLOSED
Sat, Sun; holidays; Aug

HOURS
Lunch noon–2 P.M., dinner 8–10 P.M.

RESERVATIONS
No

CREDIT CARDS
AE, MC, V

A LA CARTE
85–120F, BNC

PRIX FIXE
None

Chez l'Ami Jean
27, rue Malar (7th)

Eat well and have fun in this typical French neighborhood restaurant, complete with Mack, a big boxer dog who greets you at the door. The food is Basque, and the photos, banners, mementos, and regulars at the bar reflect the rough and tumble sports of the region.

TELEPHONE
47-05-86-89

MÉTRO
Alma-Marceau. Latour-Maubourg

OPEN
Mon–Sat lunch and dinner

CLOSED
Sun; holidays; Aug
HOURS
Lunch noon–3 P.M.,
dinner 7–10:30 P.M.
RESERVATIONS
No
CREDIT CARDS
V
A LA CARTE
110–125F, BNC
PRIX FIXE
None

Jean's menu includes all the predictable standbys found in small *quartier* spots, as well as a nice sampling of regional specialties including *pipérade*, (scrambled eggs with sweet peppers, garlic, and onions), *chiperons à la basquaise* (small squid in a rich tomato sauce), a nicely roasted chicken, and paella (sometimes this is too salty). For dessert there is a *gâteau basquaise,* a very good cream-filled cake dusted with toasted almonds. The dessert to rave over, however, is the crème caramel, which can be rather ho-hum—but here it's worth a visit to Jean's just to sample his richly smooth and satiny version, which lifts this pedestrian dish to superstar status. There's a good selection of local Basque wines, but the house red should be avoided unless you like a very strong, full-bodied wine.

La Fontaine de Mars
129, rue St-Dominique (7th)

TELEPHONE
47-05-46-44
MÉTRO
École-Militaire
OPEN
Mon–Fri lunch and dinner,
Sat lunch only
CLOSED
Sat dinner, Sun; major
holidays; Aug
HOURS
Lunch noon–2:30 P.M.,
dinner 7–9:30 P.M.
RESERVATIONS
Advised
CREDIT CARDS
V
A LA CARTE
115–130F, BNC
PRIX FIXE
Lunch only: 70F, 3 courses,
BNC

La Fontaine de Mars, owned for more than a quarter century by Paul and André Launay, is a gourmand's paradise demonstrating the popularity of French country cooking. The welcome from Mme Launay, who treats old friends and first-time visitors with the same smiling warmth; the small rooms with their cozy farmhouse feel; and strong neighborhood patronage combine to make this a reliable choice. Windowside tables look out on the square with its Fontaine de Mars, and, in summer, tables are set under the arches overlooking the square.

Do not consider coming here unless you are very hungry and in the mood for a big meal, because the portions are enormous, and you are expected to have them all, including a pitcher or bottle of wine. Overall, the simple dishes tend to be the best. The roast veal is always a winner, and so is the *fricassée de canard,* a tender piece of duck served with creamy white beans. For dessert-lovers, the *mystère chocolat,* a scoop of vanilla-bean ice cream set in a delicate meringue and surrounded by a thick chocolate sauce, is divine. The service by the matronly waitresses is always friendly, but be forewarned: the menu, handwritten daily and mimeographed in barely legible purple and red ink, is a challenge to decipher, even for the French.

La Pie Gourmande
30, rue de Bourgogne (7th)

The smells are tantalizing and the servings generous in this handkerchief-size *crêperie*, with its cozy kitchen and converted-parlor atmosphere. Open only for lunch, it fills up quickly with people from the nearby French ministries and the Musée d'Orsay, often leaving some outside waiting to get in.

The menu (which is translated into English) lists seasonal salads and every mouthwatering buckwheat crêpe you can think of and probably some you never imagined. All are not available every day, but any one listed on the blackboard menu hanging over the counter will be wonderful. I always hope *le burger*, filled with chopped beef and onions and topped with cheese *fondu* and a fried egg, will be available when I eat here. *La Natacha* is another favorite; it is filled with caviar and topped with a dollop of *crème fraîche* and a sprinkling of lemon. The Popeye pie mixes creamed spinach with eggs and melted cheese, and *l'Americaine* combines scrambled eggs and bacon. Insiders order the raspberry crêpe whenever it is on the menu, or a piece of the daily homemade cake for dessert. Don't worry—the crêpes are all light as feathers, and you can easily have two or three, or more.

TELEPHONE
45-51-32-48
MÉTRO
Assemblée Nationale
OPEN
Mon–Fri lunch
CLOSED
Dinner; Sat, Sun; major holidays; NAC
HOURS
11:30 A.M.–2:30 P.M.
RESERVATIONS
No
CREDIT CARDS
MC, V
A LA CARTE
45–65F, BNC
PRIX FIXE
None

La Poule au Pot
121, rue de l'Université (7th)

Everyone loves La Poule au Pot. With its zinc bar, shiny espresso machine, beautiful etched hanging lamps, and waiters in dark pants with long white aprons skimming their shoes, it is the kind of genuine turn-of-the-century restaurant that is rapidly disappearing in Paris.

TELEPHONE
47-05-16-36
MÉTRO
Latour-Maubourg
OPEN
Mon–Fri lunch and dinner; Sat dinner only

CLOSED
Sat lunch; Sun; holidays;
15 days in Aug
HOURS
Lunch noon–3 P.M., dinner
7:30–10:30 P.M.
RESERVATIONS
Advised
CREDIT CARDS
AE, MC, V
A LA CARTE
130–150F, BNC
PRIX FIXE
100F, 3 courses, BNC

The loyal patrons are devoted to the restaurant's outstanding tradition of good, solid, satisfying food generously served and moderately priced. The menu is varied, ranging from omelettes, fresh fish, and beef, to the daily specials. The real special here, though, is *la poule au pot*, or chicken-in-a-pot: a classic chicken stew served in its own large clay pot with a rich broth, several vegetables, and a nice chunk of pâté hiding at the bottom. Mmmmmmm good!

L'Auberge Bressane
16, avenue de la Motte-Piquet (7th)

TELEPHONE
47-05-98-37
MÉTRO
Latour-Maubourg
OPEN
Sun–Fri lunch and dinner
CLOSED
Sat; Christmas; Aug 15–Sep 15
HOURS
Lunch noon–2 P.M.,
dinner 7:30–10 P.M.
RESERVATIONS
Advised
CREDIT CARDS
DC, MC, V
A LA CARTE
140–150F, BNC
PRIX FIXE
None

Time has left its mark on the Auberge Bressane, which for over 40 years has been primly presided over by Mme Chollet and her waitresses, all dressed in black with frilly white aprons. The minute you step inside, you feel right at home. The worn planked floor, shiny copper pots, wooden lamps, hanging hams and cow bells, and masses of fresh flowers and plants create a country farmhouse atmosphere. The similarity stops there, because this is definitely a proper restaurant, with heavy cutlery, nice china, and starched linens.

The full-flavored *bonne maman* cuisine, served in big helpings to regulars not watching their waistlines, is tough to beat for pure and simple eating. You can begin with such favorites as *escargots*, (snails), *jambon de pays* (cured country ham), smoked salmon on toast, or fish soup. Then try a creamy omelette with a crisp salad, *blanquette de veau* (veal in cream), *magret de canard* (duck breast), or *poulet gratinée* (chicken in a light cream sauce with a bread crumb topping). Depending on the time of year, end the meal with a *tarte aux fraises* or *pommes* (strawberry or apple tart). When you finish, you will have had a comforting meal without ruining your budget in the process.

L'Auvergne Gourmande
127, rue St-Dominique (7th)

Blink twice and you will miss Christiane Miguel's

tiny four-table nook tucked snugly along Rue St-Dominique, only a ten-minute walk from the Eiffel Tower. The setting is homey and casual, with cooking utensils lining the walls and a radio playing in the background. The cheery welcome and good food more than make up for the tiny space and limited menu.

The restaurant is popular with students, shoppers, and neighborhood women, one of whom told me that it is one of her favorite lunch spots because the food is delicious. She is right—it *is* delicious. The a la carte menu offers several nice salads, a plate of cold meats, a daily hot dish, and homemade desserts, including a devastatingly rich chocolate fudge cake. Everything is made fresh each morning, and the daily specials and desserts go quickly, so to avoid disappointment, plan to go early for the best selection.

TELEPHONE
47-05-60-79

MÉTRO
École-Militaire

OPEN
Mon–Fri lunch

CLOSED
Dinner; Sat, Sun; NAC

HOURS
Noon–4 P.M.

RESERVATIONS
No

CREDIT CARDS
None

A LA CARTE
50–70F, BNC

PRIX FIXE
None

Le Bistrot de Breteuil
3, place de Breteuil (7th)

This recently revamped restaurant has what is takes: great Parisian atmosphere, attentive service, reasonable prices, and reliable food—every time you go. Le Bistrot de Breteuil, not too far from Les Invalides, also has one of the most beautiful dining terraces in Paris. Wrapped around an entire corner of the Place de Breuteuil, the open and airy glassed-in restaurant hosts a *branché* crowd that makes elegance look easy. The tables are beautifully set with crisp white linens and fresh flowers, and teams of traditionally outfitted waiters serve with precision and aplomb.

The 162F prix fixe menu includes the house aperitif (a sparkling white wine *kir*) and eight or nine seasonal choices for the *entrée, plat,* and dessert, *plus* a half-bottle of wine and coffee. By Paris standards, this bargain is on the A list, so plan accordingly and reserve before you go.

TELEPHONE
45-67-07-27

MÉTRO
Duroc, Sèvres-Lecourbe

OPEN
Daily lunch and dinner

CLOSED
Never; NAC

HOURS
Lunch noon–2:30 P.M., dinner 7:15–10:30 P.M.

RESERVATIONS
Necessary

CREDIT CARDS
MC, V

A LA CARTE
None

PRIX FIXE
16F, 3 courses including aperitif, wine, and coffee

Le Mâconnais
19, rue du Bac (7th)

TELEPHONE
42-61-21-89
MÉTRO
Rue du Bac
OPEN
Mon–Fri lunch and dinner,
Sat dinner only
CLOSED
Sat lunch, Sun; holidays; 1
week in Feb and at Christmas;
3 weeks in Aug
HOURS
Lunch noon–2:30 P.M., dinner
7–10:30 P.M.
RESERVATIONS
Advised, especially for lunch
CREDIT CARDS
MC, V
A LA CARTE
140–160F, BNC
PRIX FIXE
None

The service in this appealing bistro near the Musée d'Orsay is notable, the setting animated, and the welcome from *la patronne*, Mme Lefebure, genuine. At lunch an energetic, chic crowd turns Le Mâconnais into a sea of enthusiasm and activity, so if you are not up to calculated confusion, go for dinner when time is not so much of the essence, and the pace will be more leisurely.

The food is always right on the mark, the mouthwatering specialties served with style. The chef shows his mastery with heritage recipes of *fricassée d' escargots*, a sturdy *jambonneau aux lentilles*, and a supremely tender *poulet à la creme*. The ultimate finales to remember are the *marquise au chocolate* and the slightly tart *gratin des fruits*.

Le Petit Niçois
10, rue Amélie (7th)

TELEPHONE
45-51-83-65
MÉTRO
Latour-Maubourg
OPEN
Tues–Sat lunch and dinner,
Mon dinner only
CLOSED
Mon lunch, Sun; major
holidays; Aug
HOURS
Lunch noon–2 P.M.,
dinner 7–10:30 P.M.
RESERVATIONS
Advised
CREDIT CARDS
MC, V
A LA CARTE
180F, BNC
PRIX FIXE
148F, 3 courses, BNC

Over and over again, neighborhood residents will tell you that Le Petit Niçois is one of the best quality-and-value-for-the-money restaurants in the *quartier*. For my dining franc, and for that of many readers who have written to me after eating here, the residents are absolutely correct—it is terrific!

Le Petit Niçois is a tiny two-level family-run restaurant filled to the brim with a noisy mixed crowd including crews from the TV news shows who broadcast from the nearby studios. If you want meat, delicate soufflés, or *nouvelle cuisine*, look elsewhere. The specialty here is fish, fish, and more fish. Owner-chef Rolan Rulos makes some of the best bouillabaise served on the banks of the Seine, and his paella, served only on Thursdays and Saturdays, is worth a special trip. For perfectly grilled jumbo shrimp, fresh lobster, a delicate *sole belle meunière*, and a simple but exquisite poached turbot, eat here. The desserts always look good, but after the gargantuan main course, no one ever has much room for anything more than a cool *sorbet* or a chocolate mousse.

Le Petit Tronquet
28, rue de l'Exposition (7th)

Look no further, here it is: that perfect, romantic little Parisian restaurant, tucked away on a back street that only *you* have discovered. Le Petit Tronquet is not far from the Eiffel Tower and just off Rue St-Dominique, the *quartier's* premier shopping street. Inside, marble-topped bistro tables with linen cloths and a vase of dried flowers fill a room decorated with assorted paintings, posters, fringed lamps, and flea market memorabilia. The entire effect is one of comfortable and quiet intimacy. The food is all purchased and prepared by Patrick Vessière and nicely served by his attractive wife. The *only* thing to consider when dining here is the prix fixe menu, which is an absolute steal when you consider the quality it represents. Every day there are three different *entrées*, *plats*, and desserts. You might start with homemade ravioli stuffed with *chèvre*, or a copious salad laced with herbs and finely minced shallots. All the *plats* are attractively garnished with fresh vegetables and pan-roasted potatoes. The desserts are all made here, including the creamy nougat ice cream. Wines from small wineries throughout France are featured each month.

TELEPHONE
47-05-80-39

MÉTRO
École-Militaire

OPEN
Mon–Fri lunch and dinner, Sat dinner only

CLOSED
Sat lunch, Sun; holidays; 15 days in Aug

HOURS
Lunch noon–3 P.M., dinner 7–10:30 P.M.

RESERVATIONS
Advised, especially on weekends

CREDIT CARDS
V

A LA CARTE
140F, BNC

PRIX FIXE
100F, 3 courses, BNC

Le Relais Saint-Germain
190, boulevard St-Germain (7th)

Offering a prix fixe menu of great variety and imagination, Le Relais Saint-Germain has been a success since the day it opened. Recognizing the impressive food value offered, Parisians return here often for enlightened cooking served with professional savoir faire in lovely air-conditioned surroundings.

The four-course menu, complete with house red or white wine, headlines at least 11 *entrées* including fresh melon and Parma ham, grilled spring vegetables

TELEPHONE
42-22-21-35, 45-48-11-73

MÉTRO
St-Germain-des-Prés, Rue du Bac

OPEN
Daily lunch and dinner

CLOSED
Never; NAC

HOURS
Lunch 12:30–2:30 P.M., dinner 7:30–11 P.M.

RESERVATIONS
Yes
CREDIT CARDS
MC, V
A LA CARTE
None
PRIX FIXE
180F, 4 courses, BC

with olive oil and basil, and a rich foie gras served on toast points. There are 14 main-dish offerings such as *foie de veau au vinaigre de cidre* (liver), *magret de canard* (duck breast), *cassoulet,* and grilled beef *filet* steak. After a choice of Brie or *chèvre* cheese and an irresistible selection of desserts, you will agree with your fellow diners: *c'est magnifique!*

Le Sancerre
22, avenue Rapp (7th)

TELEPHONE
45-51-75-91
MÉTRO
Alma-Marceau, École-Militaire
OPEN
Mon–Sat
CLOSED
Sun; holidays; NAC
HOURS
Mon–Fri 7:30 A.M.–8:30 P.M.,
Sat 8:30 A.M.–4 P.M.;
continuous service
RESERVATIONS
Yes, between 12:30 and 2 P.M.
CREDIT CARDS
MC, V
A LA CARTE
50–90F, BNC
PRIX FIXE
None

Le Sancerre is one of my favorite wine bars in Paris. The menu is short, but the food and wine always rate an A+ with the nonstop flow of regulars who have made it a fashionable spot to lunch in this part of the seventh arrondissement. Past the rather somber exterior you will find yourself in pleasant, rustic surroundings with comforting kitchen sounds and smells floating by. This is the place for a creamy herb or cheese omelette with a side of golden pan-fried potatoes and a crisp green salad. Or, for the more adventurous, a spicy *andouillette* made with Sancerre wine, or a *crotin de Chafignon,* the sharp goat cheese that goes perfectly with a glass or two of Sancerre. While waiting for your meal, baskets of the famous Poilâne bread and crocks of sweet butter are brought to the table. Your wine, of course, will be Sancerre.

Note: If you appreciate Art Nouveau architecture, take a close look at the facade of the building directly across the street at 29, avenue Rapp, constructed in 1901 by the architect Lavirotle. Then turn right and walk to the post office at No. 37. At the end of the dead-end street by the post office are more lovely doorways and ornate latticework.

L'Oeillade
10, rue St-Simon (7th)

TELEPHONE
42-22-01-60
MÉTRO
Rue du Bac

Parisians are pushing aside the fussy, contrived meals of *nouvelle cuisine* and in its place lapping up rib-sticking bistro fare. Nowhere is this more appar-

prising that most major museums in Paris have some sort of restaurant. The best of these by far is the Palais d'Orsay, situated in the Musée d'Orsay. Here diners sit in wide wicker armchairs in a massive Belle Époque dining room with magnificent frescoed ceilings by the 19th-century painter Gabriel Ferrier. Marble statues, gilt-framed mirrors, sparkling chandeliers, and sprays of fresh flowers complete the spectacular room. Fortunately, the food is as impressive as the decor. At first glance, you might think the prices would be too, but they are not, especially *la formule rapide.* This bargain meal features a beautiful buffet with a variety of salads, vegetables, cold meats, and fish followed by a choice of four desserts and a pitcher of wine. Also available are moderately priced *entrées* and main courses and a full range of desserts to go with afternoon tea.

Note: There is a nonsmoking area.

MÉTRO
Solférino

OPEN
Tues–Sun lunch and tea; Thurs dinner only

CLOSED
Mon all day; Tues, Wed, Fri–Sun for dinner; NAC

HOURS
Lunch 11:30 A.M.–2:30 P.M., afternoon tea 4–5:30 P.M., dinner (Thurs only) 7–9:30 P.M.

RESERVATIONS
For large groups

CREDIT CARDS
MC, V

A LA CARTE
130F, BNC

PRIX FIXE
Lunch only: 70F, *"la formule rapide,"* buffet, and dessert; BC

EIGHTH ARRONDISSEMENT

This is an area of splendor, elegance, money, and classic images of Paris, especially the view of the Champs-Élysées from the Arc de Triomphe to the Place de la Concorde. Shoppers with impressive bank balances ply the haute couture luxury shops along the Avenues Marceau and Montaigne and on the Rue du Faubourg St-Honoré. Gourmets and gourmands make pilgrimages to Fauchon, the world's most famous grocery store, and tourists go to Maxim's, the one-time shrine for fine dining in Paris. The area is alive and bustling during the weekdays, but on holidays and weekends, it is deserted.

Note: The most famous boulevard in the world, with its myriad sidewalk cafés filled with pretty young women, is very deceptive. No true Parisian would ever seriously dine on the Champs-Élysées, any more than any true New Yorker would head for Times Square to have a fine meal. The places along the Champs-Élysées serve inferior food, are crowded with tourists, and are always overpriced. Of course, sitting in a café along the Champs-Élysées and enjoying a drink *is* Paris. But, for a real increase in value and quality of food, walk one or two blocks on either side of the boulevard.

EIGHTH ARRONDISSEMENT RESTAURANTS

American Pershing Hall	L'Assiette Lyonnaise
Chez Mélanie	Le Boccador
City Rock Café	L'Écluse (François 1ᵉʳ)
Fauchon	L'Écluse (Madeleine)
La Boutique à	Le Roi du Pot-au-Feu
Sandwichs	Le Val d'Isère à Paris
Ladurée Tea Room and	Lina's Sandwiches
Patisserie	Lunchtime
La Fermette Marbeuf	Peny
1900	Restaurant Germain

American Pershing Hall
49, rue Pierre Charron (8th)

Whatever your dining needs may be, chances are they'll be met at American Pershing Hall, a dignified dining room in the former American Legion Hall. Here you can eat breakfast, brunch, lunch, and dinner, and have tea while reading through the newsletters and pamphlets put out by the American community in Paris. Or you can arrange to have a cocktail party, a reunion, or a child's birthday party catered. When I first went, I expected it to be overrun with American tourists and war veterans. I was delighted to see more berets than baseball caps at the nicely appointed linen-covered tables in the two formal dining rooms and on the covered terrace.

The food is good and the prices fair, *if* you stay with the prix fixe menus, which feature traditional French dishes. Once you begin to wander, the final bill could add up to more than your budget would like. If you're not in the mood for French food, you can still stay within your budget by ordering the paella, chili con carne, or *fondu mexicaine*, all served for two persons.

TELEPHONE
42-25-81-22, 42-25-38-17

MÉTRO
Franklin D. Roosevelt

OPEN
Daily

CLOSED
Never; NAC

HOURS
8:30 A.M.–midnight, continuous service

RESERVATIONS
Not necessary

CREDIT CARDS
AE, DC, MC, V

A LA CARTE
210F, BNC

PRIX FIXE
Lunch: 59F, 3 courses, BNC; 85F, 3 courses, BNC; 130F, 3 courses (wider selection), BNC; 150F, 3 courses (wider selection), BC (includes *kir*); Children's menu: 50F, 3 courses, BC; dinner: 85F, 3 courses, BNC; 130F, 3 courses (wider selection) BNC; 150F, 3 courses (wider selection), BC (includes a *kir*); Sat and Sun brunch: 80F, 100F, 120F, 150F; BC (price depends on number of selections)

Chez Mélanie
27, rue de Colisée (8th)

Here's a great Cheap Eat in Paris, but if you don't know about it beforehand, you will *never* find it. Chez Mélanie is only a minute or two away from the Champs-Élysées and is perhaps the best bargain-lunch bet in the heart of this expensive section of Paris. To reach it, you enter off Rue de Colisée and go through the door at the end of the first courtyard. Walk through the second courtyard, and climb the 60 steep steps on your right. In the 1920s Chez Mélanie was the lunch canteen for the seamstresses working for the *couturières* in the garment district. Nothing much has changed, and today it still looks like a boardinghouse dining room, with its hard chairs, harsh lighting, and steamy windows. But—

TELEPHONE
43-59-42-76

MÉTRO
St-Philippe-du-Roule

OPEN
Mon–Fri lunch only

CLOSED
Dinner; Sat, Sun; holidays; NAC

HOURS
Lunch 11:30 A.M.–3 P.M.

RESERVATIONS
No

CREDIT CARDS
None

A LA CARTE
None

PRIX FIXE
50F, 3 courses, BC

the philanthropic price is amazing and the food is worth the hike.

Fifty diners usually are squeezed into two rooms, selecting from a back-to-basics menu that costs only 50F for three courses and a quarter-liter of wine. There is a choice of three or four starters, two daily specials, or a steak. The steak is tough, so it's best to stick with one of the specials. Then you have a choice of cheese or a simple dessert of fresh-fruit compote, ice cream, or a slice of homemade fruit *tarte*. When you have finished your meal, you will be able to spend the rest of the day well satisfied that for your food franc, you have just had one of the best buys in Paris.

City Rock Café
13, rue de Berri (8th)

TELEPHONE
43-59-52-09

MÉTRO
George-V

OPEN
Daily

CLOSED
Never; NAC

HOURS
Noon–2:30 A.M., continuous service; live music every night

RESERVATIONS
No

CREDIT CARDS
MC, V

A LA CARTE
65–100F, BNC

PRIX FIXE
Sunday brunch: 110F, includes juice and coffee

Welcome to the City Rock Café, Paris's grand-scale Hollywood-style restaurant serving *cuisine à l'Americain*. Warning: City Rock Cafe is *not* for anyone looking for quiet, discreet, exclusive surroundings. It *is* for those wanting to check out *le dernier cri* in hair, accessories, clothes, and entertainment. The food is almost secondary to all of this, but manages to hold its own despite the electric surroundings in this virtual supermarket of rock and roll. Inside, the sheer volume and space is exciting and visually overwhelming, and fun is the main event for the hip under-40 crowd who have made this one of the *trés chic* spots to be near the Champs-Élysées.

Elvis's pink Cadillac is on the right of the entrance. Bessie the cow hangs upside down from the ceiling. A stuffed dress that once belonged to Marilyn Monroe adorns one wall; old automobile license plates and antique film posters crowd others. The waitresses are dressed in the finest of the fifties; clown, balloons, and videos for all ages make Sundays really something; and over it all great rock-and-roll hits blare at hearing-impairing decibel levels from the jukeboxes or the live rock band playing in the disco in the evening. All this is just two minutes from the Champs-Élysées, so stop by for a drink, a bowl of chili, a plate of quesadillas, or an outrageous banana split. Or try it for Sunday brunch and bring the kids. It's hard to match this one; you have to see it to believe it.

Fauchon
26, place de la Madeleine (8th)

In 1886 Auguste Fauchon opened his *épicerie fine* on the Place de la Madeleine. The rest is history. Today, a visit to Fauchon, the most famous gourmet grocery store in the world, is one of the must-see spots in Paris. With its magnificent museum-quality window displays and mind-boggling selections of more than 30,000 gastronomical goodies, Fauchon is the epitome of what a gourmet grocery store should be.

The energetic new president of Fauchon, Martine Premat, has polished the image even further by remodeling the old stand-up cafeteria into a magnificent bakery and candy store. Next door is a three-level building containing a rooftop garden restaurant and piano bar (wildly expensive), an expanded grocery carrying almost every known type of tea, coffee, spice, and herb, as well as a line of Fauchon china, crystal, and tableware. The Cheap Eater destination here is the basement cafeteria and rotisserie. For a quick lunch, a mid-morning cup of great coffee (and only 5F to 6F) or an afternoon snack, this spot is a sure thing. Here cafeteria dining is given new meaning with specials and regular offerings prepared using only the finest ingredients from Fauchon's. All the food is surprisingly reasonable, and the service is *fast,* a real bonus for the hungry traveler on the run. Keep in mind that the cafeteria is packed solid during the lunch hour, so early arrivals always have the best selection.

TELEPHONE
47-42-60-11

MÉTRO
Madeleine

OPEN
Mon–Sat

CLOSED
Sun; holidays; NAC

HOURS
8:30 A.M.–7 P.M., continuous service (until selections run out); lunch 11:30 A.M.–2 P.M.

RESERVATIONS
No

CREDIT CARDS
AE, DC, MC, V

A LA CARTE
30–85F, BNC

PRIX FIXE
None

La Boutique à Sandwichs
12, rue du Colisée (8th)

Where shall we eat before going to see a film on the Champs-Élysées? Finding a reasonable place to

TELEPHONE
43-59-56-69

MÉTRO
Franklin D. Roosevelt
OPEN
Mon–Sat
CLOSED
Sun; 3 weeks in August
HOURS
11:30 A.M.–1 A.M., continuous
service
RESERVATIONS
No
CREDIT CARDS
V
A LA CARTE
45–100F, BNC
PRIX FIXE
None

eat in this area has always been an up-hill project. No longer. Not if you know about Hubert and Claude Schick's Boutique à Sandwichs, only a half block from this famous street.

Similar to a New York deli, La Boutique is paradise for any sandwich-lover. In addition to more than 50 sandwiches of all types and sizes, they serve *raclette*, omelettes, salads, and steaks. The best advice is to avoid these, and stick to what they do best: sandwiches. Sit at the counter, order a cool beer, a rare roast beef or a warm corned beef on *pain Poilâne*, and savor one of the best answers to fast food Paris has to offer.

Ladurée Tea Room and Pâtisserie
16, rue Royale (8th)

TELEPHONE
42-60-21-79
MÉTRO
Madeleine, Concorde
OPEN
Mon–Sat
CLOSED
Sun; holidays; Aug
HOURS
8:30 A.M.–7 P.M., continuous
service; hot meals 11:30 A.M.–
3 P.M.
RESERVATIONS
For lunch on 1st floor
CREDIT CARDS
V
A LA CARTE
40–110F, BC
PRIX FIXE
None

Ladurée boasts some of Paris's most delectable pastries, served by some of the rudest, most unpleasant waitresses you ever will encounter. If you can overcome the behavior of the staff, who admittedly are overworked and probably underpaid, this is a superb site for a nicely prepared hot lunch, a creamy omelette with a crisp green salad, a delicious teatime snack, or a flaky breakfast croissant and a cup of the very best café au lait. Blue ribbons in the dessert category go to their *royals*, almond-flavored macaroon cookies filled with chocolate, mocha, or vanilla cream. Once sampled they are unforgettable. The downstairs seating is around postage-stamp-sized tables, under a pastel ceiling mural of chubby cherubs performing all sorts of baking duties. Here you can watch the hustle and bustle of the well-dressed crowds standing ten-deep at the pastry counter. For lunch, it is much more comfortable to reserve a table upstairs, where the atmosphere is rather solemn, but the scene is less hectic.

La Fermette Marbeuf 1900
5, rue Marbeuf (8th)

TELEPHONE
47-23-31-31

Of the many Belle Époque restaurants flourishing

in Paris today, this one is exceptional. For the best experience of it, reserve a table in the *jardin d'hiver*, a spectacular glass-roofed winter garden featuring Art Nouveau grill-work, 5,000 elaborate faïence tiles, and beautiful leaded-glass windows with intricate floral designs. This room was purchased in total from the Maisons-Lafitte and installed as the *premiére salle* at La Fermette Marbeuf. The restaurant was declared a national historic monument in 1983.

Fortunately, the breathtaking decor does not overshadow the food. The cuisine is highlighted by exquisite seasonal *entrées*. The culinary cornerstones of beef tournedos, leg of lamb, and innovative fish preparations, plus a host of artistic dessert dishes, round out the lengthy menu. The best dining value is the four-course dinner menu with a choice of two starters including a *terrine de foies de volaille*, (chicken liver terrine), and two *plats*, followed by a cheese course and their *gâteau fondant à l'americain*, a decadently rich fudge cake.

There is no music, and the rooms are too large and brightly lit to be ideal for an intimate dinner, but La Fermette is close to the Champs-Élysées and is a very pleasing formal dining experience, especially on Sunday when so many other restaurants are closed.

MÉTRO
Alma-Marceau

OPEN
Daily lunch and dinner

CLOSED
Never; NAC

HOURS
Lunch noon–3 P.M.,
dinner 7:30–11:30 P.M.

RESERVATIONS
Yes

CREDIT CARDS
AE, DC, MC, V

A LA CARTE
250–280F, BNC

PRIX FIXE
150F, 4 courses, BNC

L'Assiette Lyonnaise
21, rue Marbeuf (8th)

The prices are too cheap to ignore, the red and white interior is adorable, and the restaurant has the advantage of being open on Sunday for both lunch and dinner as well as until 11:30 P.M. for dinner daily. However, the menu is limited to the Lyonnaise specialties of *andouillettes*, (chitterling sausages), tripe, sausage, and three plats du jour featuring heavy-duty pork, *bavettes*, and fish on Friday.

This isn't to say that what they do at L'Assiette Lyonnaise is not delicious, because it is—*if* you are geared for mountains of waist-expanding food.

Their desserts follow suit with such temptingly

TELEPHONE
47-20-94-80

MÉTRO
Franklin D. Roosevelt

OPEN
Daily lunch and dinner

CLOSED
Never; NAC

HOURS
Lunch noon–3 P.M.,
dinner 7–11:30 P.M.

RESERVATIONS
No

CREDIT CARDS
MC, V

A LA CARTE
120F, BNC

rich selections as *tarte Tatin,* chocolate cake, and *crème brûlée.*

Le Boccador
7, rue Boccador (8th)

TELEPHONE
47-23-57-80
MÉTRO
Franklin D. Roosevelt, Alma-Marceau
OPEN
Mon–Sat lunch and dinner
CLOSED
Sun; holidays; NAC
HOURS
Lunch noon–3 P.M., dinner 7 P.M.–midnight
RESERVATIONS
Yes
CREDIT CARDS
AE, DC, MC, V
A LA CARTE
170–190F, BNC
PRIX FIXE
None

From my mail, I know that no one is ever disappointed after dining at Le Boccador, which continues to be a special find for foot-weary visitors from the Champs-Élysées. Its cozy bar and traditional French food served at well-spaced tables have made it a mainstay for the faithful in this fashionable neighborhood. In the summer, sidewalk tables set under the awnings add a further dining dimension. Excellent service is provided by friendly waiters clad in white shirts, black pants, and maroon vests festooned with buttons and badges given to them by customers.

The dishes are always-reliable French seasonal standards served without a *nouvelle* kiwi in sight. Best bets include the daily fresh fish offerings, the veal medallions in mustard sauce, and the tender baby lamb garnished with potatoes *dauphine* for two. During the fall game season, don't miss the roast pheasant or the venison served with two vegetable purees. The desserts range from *tartes* and *profiteroles* to iced Grând Marnier soufflé and a *crème brûlée* one diner described as "the size of a Frisbee." As is everything else, all desserts are prepared with great care and served with style.

L'Écluse (François 1er)
64, rue François 1er (8th)
Telephone: 47-20-77-09
Métro: Franklin D. Roosevelt

See page 42.

L'Écluse (Madeleine)
15, place de la Madeleine (8th)
Telephone: 42-65-34-69
Métro: Madeleine
Open: Mon–Sat

Closed: Sun; NAC
Hours: Noon–12:30 A.M., continuous service

See page 42.

Le Roi du Pot-au-Feu
40, rue du Ponthieu (8th)

It is easy to imagine little French *grand'mères* cooking in the kitchens of these two restaurants, which are monuments to one of the tastiest French peasant dishes, pot-au-feu. Places are set at wooden tables with red and white checked tablecloths. To keep your shirt front clean, ask for one of the large bibs.

Pay no attention to anything else on the short menu and concentrate only on their timeless specialty. Much lighter than its Anglo-American cousin, beef stew, pot-au-feu is served at Le Roi in two courses. The first is an earthenware pot of steaming broth. The second consists of the meat, vegetables, and bone marrow flavored with herbs and sea salt that have been slowly simmering in the broth for hours. This is served with pickles, sharp mustard, and fresh bread. Enjoy your pot-au-feu with a nice Gamay wine and have a good sticky piece of the *tarte Tatin* for dessert. After dessert, order a glass of *grand-père's* home-brewed Calvados, and you won't soon forget this meal.

TELEPHONE
43-59-41-62

MÉTRO
Franklin D. Roosevelt

OPEN
Mon–Sat

CLOSED
Sun; holidays; mid-July to Mid-August

HOURS
Noon–10 P.M., continuous service

RESERVATIONS
No

CREDIT CARDS
MC, V

A LA CARTE
125F, BNC

PRIX FIXE
160F, 3 courses (coffee and half bottle of wine included)

Le Val d'Isère à Paris
2, rue de Berri (8th)

Antique wooden skis on the walls, a bar made of skis, and terrific old photos of famous skiers from the Val d'Isère region of southeastern France dominate the interior of this rather large restaurant, located only a half block from the clip joints along the Champs-Élysées.

This is always a lively spot, thanks to an affable owner and an alert staff. Neighborhood businesspeople and families can usually be found sitting by the open sidewalk windows, greeting friends as they pass by. Big and ugly, but oh, so comfortable red and brown Naugahyde-covered chairs make it a little

TELEPHONE
43-59-12-66

MÉTRO
George-V

OPEN
Daily

CLOSED
Aug

HOURS
Noon–1:30 P.M., continuous service

RESERVATIONS
From 12:30–3 P.M.; no reservations accepted after 8 P.M.

CREDIT CARDS
MC, V
A LA CARTE
120–190F, BNC
PRIX FIXE
None

crowded during the peak hours, and some stepping over and shuffling are required to get everyone seated at the Formica-topped tables, but the effort during the crunch is well worth it.

The menu consistently delivers sound French food from noon until past midnight 365 days a year. This is a good place to bring children for family favorites of spaghetti, thick onion soup, a *croque-monsieur*, or a plate of ham and fried eggs. These, along with the roast chicken, lamb chops, steaks, ice cream creations, and a full range of fresh oysters, Burgundy, and Savoie fondues are served in lumberjack portions.

Lina's Sandwiches
8, rue Marbeuf (8th)

Telephone: 47-23-92-33
Métro: Franklin D. Roosevelt
Open: Mon–Sat
Closed: Sun; holidays; NAC

See page 55.

Lunchtime
255, rue St-Honoré (8th)

TELEPHONE
42-60-80-40
MÉTRO
Concorde
OPEN
Mon–Sat
CLOSED
Sun; holidays; NAC
HOURS
11 A.M.–4 P.M., continuous service
RESERVATIONS
No
CREDIT CARDS
None
A LA CARTE
25–50F, BNC
PRIX FIXE
None

Its wide variety of well-stacked sandwiches and fresh salads have made Lunchtime a favorite haunt of secretaries, smart tourists, and cute young things in the area of the fashionable Rue St-Honoré. This one is easy to miss, because it's hidden in a courtyard. Look for the sign sitting alongside the entryway to the courtyard at No. 255 Rue St-Honoré. The inside is spacious and nicely done with murals of Cape Cod and interesting displays of big seashells, sailor's knots, and sailing artifacts.

You can select from a list of 24 sandwiches served on crusty *pain complet, pain de campagne,* or pita bread. The list of fillings range from cheese to combinations of turkey, ham, beef, chicken, fish, and vegetables. Six or seven salads and an alluring lineup of desserts complete the dining picture. Everything can be eaten here at comfortable tables, or packed to go.

If you take your sandwich with you, it will cost a few francs less.

Peny
3, place de la Madeleine (8th)

In a neighborhood known for restaurants serving 500F and 600F lunches, Peny is a plush, but inexpensive alternative. The food is reliable, and the interior is clean, comfortable, and filled every day with an attractively stylish crowd. The brightly upholstered chairs on the sidewalk terrace offer some of the best people-watching in this part of Paris.

A wide variety of café food is offered. One long-standing favorite is the *poulet à la crème* (boned chicken breast on toast, smothered with a delicate cream sauce and served piping hot on a platter). The only dessert to consider is the *gâteau à la noix de coco* (a feathery light coconut cake).

Naturally, a restaurant cannot be recommended only for its toilets, but it's good to know that Peny's are clean, tiled, and have separate sinks and perfumed liquid soap. If you have spent the morning hoofing it around the Tuileries, the Jeu de Paume, and the Madeleine Church, or visiting the boutiques that line Rue St-Honoré, this is a good place to freshen up, have a sensible meal, and relax inside, or outside under the shade of umbrellas and sycamore trees while enjoying a wide-angle view of Parisian life.

TELEPHONE
42-65-06-75

MÉTRO
Madeleine

OPEN
Daily

CLOSED
Never; NAC

HOURS
7 A.M.–10 P.M., continuous service; breakfast 7–11 A.M.; lunch noon–3 P.M.; hot and cold snacks and pastries 3–10 P.M.

RESERVATIONS
No

CREDIT CARDS
MC, V

A LA CARTE
25–80F, BNC

PRIX FIXE
None

Restaurant Germain
19, rue Jean Mermoz (8th)

We're talking Cheap Eats here, not Maxim's, so don't expect starched linens, fine wines, soft music, and haute cuisine served by heel-clicking waiters anticipating your every whim. You *can* expect, however, some mighty good home cooking in this bare-bones restaurant not far from the Champs-Élysées.

The food can best be described as meat-based and rich: sheer heaven for red meat fans, but not for dieters or semi-veggies. At lunch, you will see serious

TELEPHONE
43-59-29-24

MÉTRO
St-Philippe de Roule

OPEN
Mon–Fri

CLOSED
Sat, Sun; holidays; Aug

HOURS
Lunch noon–2:30 P.M., dinner 7–9:30 P.M.

RESERVATIONS
No

CREDIT CARDS
V

A LA CARTE
140F, BNC

PRIX FIXE
None

diners warming up on a salad of *chèvre chaud* followed by coq au vin or a rich *côte de veau Normande* (veal chop in cream). They usually wind up with a simple chocolate mousse or the fruit charlotte. In the evening, Germain fills up quickly with working couples, professionals, and other thrifty-minded French who know how to eat well while paying less.

NINTH ARRONDISSEMENT

The ninth is predominantly a business area, with many banks, head offices of corporations, law firms, and insurance companies. The Grands Boulevards, laid out by Baron Haussmann, are those wide thoroughfares that lead from the Opéra to Place de la République. The smart end is at the Opéra, the center of Paris during the Belle Époque, that period of elegance and gaiety characterizing Parisian life from the mid–19th century to World War I.

NINTH ARRONDISSEMENT
Right Bank: Grands
Boulevards, *grand magazins*
(Au Printemps and Galéries
Lafayette), the Opéra

NINTH ARRONDISSEMENT RESTAURANTS

Casa Miguel
Chartier-Montmarte
Jeremy's Sandwich &
   Coffee Shop
Le Relais Savoyard
Le Roi du Pot-au-Feu
Tea Follies
Verdeau–La Pomme de
   Terre Gourmande

Casa Miguel
48, rue St-Georges (9th)

WARNING: This restaurant is included for those who delight in collecting unusual dining experiences and expect to get *only* what they pay for.

The sign on the door reads, "Eat Better, Save Money," and you will certainly save money at Casa Miguel. Mme Maria Codina, now in her eighties, holds the *Guinness Book of World Records* award for having the cheapest restaurant in the Western Hemisphere. Her three-course, five-franc meals include house red wine shared from a bottle at the table. Because she does all the work herself, hygiene standards may not always be up to the American ideal. She never loses her patience as she hurries around in her faded print housedress and apron, clucking at her patrons like a mother hen.

She sets only 32 places twice a day for lunch and dinner, and serves you on oilcloth-covered tables. There are no reservations and no second seatings, so you must time your arrival to beat the line that forms

TELEPHONE
None

MÉTRO
St-Georges

OPEN
Mon–Sat lunch and dinner, Sun lunch only

CLOSED
Sun dinner; 1 week in late July or early Aug

HOURS
Lunch noon–1 P.M., dinner 7–8 P.M.

RESERVATIONS
No

CREDIT CARDS
None

A LA CARTE
None

PRIX FIXE
5F, 3 courses, BC

at the door. She offers pâté or salad for the first course, and solid main dishes such as couscous, white beans with mutton, Toulouse sausage, pork chops, macaroni, fish, and chicken with rice. The last course is usually a piece of fresh fruit or cheese. If you do not want the main course on the menu, you can pay an additional 4F and get one of the other *plats*. Seconds on dessert or cheese will set you back another 1.50F.

Chartier-Montmartre
7, rue de Faubourg Montmartre (9th)
Telephone: 47-70-86-29
Métro: Montmartre

See page 50.

Jeremy's Sandwich & Coffee Shop
43, rue Fontaine (9th)

TELEPHONE
42-80-30-80
MÉTRO
Blanche
OPEN
Mon–Sat
CLOSED
Sun; NAC
HOURS
9 A.M.–2 A.M.,
continuous service
RESERVATIONS
No
CREDIT CARDS
None
A LA CARTE
40–50F, BC
PRIX FIXE
None

Olivier Amiot confidently claims that he makes some of the best sandwiches in Paris. The key is his closely guarded recipe for the baguettes and whole grain rolls he bakes daily. He encourages diners to sample sandwiches filled with avocado and crab, smoked salmon and cucumber, roast beef, cheese and *crudités*, and his pièce de resistance, the *banane spécialité maison*: toasted bread topped with bananas, chocolate, and rum. Try it; it is really something. In addition there are daily quiches, salads, cold meat platters, thick milk shakes, and fresh fruit juices, squeezed while you wait. Everything can be eaten here or packaged to go.

While you are here, feast your eyes on the changing art exhibitions and the unique sculpted coffee machine created in honor of the working women in the neighborhood, which is Pigalle. This is Paris's red light district and full of everything you can possibly imagine—and lots you might not want to.

Le Relais Savoyard
13, rue Rodier (9th)

TELEPHONE
45-26-17-48

Le Relais Savoyard is a wonderful example of the

French tradition of family-run bistros, bustling with middle-aged waitresses and a happy, almost exclusively neighborhood crowd. Overall it is not sophisticated, but for blue-collar working-class atmosphere and a Cheap Eat as well, it is just the ticket.

The timeless menu is a collection of homey dishes from the Savoie region of France. On a wintery evening it is nice to sit in the wood-paneled room in back, which is lined with the owners' collection of antique coffeepots and sauce dishes, and order the *côte de veau maison*, a rich combination of veal, ham, mushrooms, and cheese, topped with Mornay sauce and flambéed. If you go with a group, either of the fondue specialties makes a satisfying choice.

Desserts tend to be an afterthought on the part of the chef, so it is better to concentrate on the rest of the meal.

MÉTRO
Notre-Dame de Lorette, Anvers

OPEN
Mon–Sat lunch, dinner, and bar

CLOSED
Sun; holidays; 10 days in winter; a few days in May; Aug

HOURS
Lunch noon–2:30 P.M., dinner 7:30–10 P.M.; bar open all day

RESERVATIONS
No

CREDIT CARDS
MC, V

A LA CARTE
110–125F, BC

PRIX FIXE
75F, 3 courses, BC; 105F, 3 courses, BC

Le Roi du Pot-au-Feu
34, rue Vignon (9th)
Telephone: 47-42-37-10
Métro: Madeleine, Havre-Caumartin

See page 117.

Tea Follies
6, place Gustave Toudouze (9th)

First-time visitors to Paris generally don't stray far from the beaten track. This is too bad, because they miss some of the most interesting places that way. Not too far from Montmartre and a number of small theaters is Tea Follies, a casual spot that is a favorite with actors and a fat gray cat named Justine. It is a welcome place to relax after looking through the antique shops and funky clothing boutiques around Place St-Georges. When I go, I order the tangy lemon-curd *tarte* or the *ardechois*, a fattening delight made with chocolate and chestnuts, and spend a lazy hour leafing through the English and French periodicals stacked about. On warm afternoons, the cobblestone terrace is the place to sit and nibble on raisin

TELEPHONE
42-80-08-44

MÉTRO
St-Georges

OPEN
Daily

CLOSED
Evenings in winter; Christmas Day, New Year's Day; NAC

HOURS
Mon–Sat 9 A.M.–9 P.M., Sun 9 A.M.–7 P.M.; breakfast 9 A.M.– noon, lunch noon–closing, tea 3 P.M.–closing, Sun brunch noon–4 P.M.

RESERVATIONS
No

CREDIT CARDS
V

A LA CARTE
50–100F, BNC

PRIX FIXE
Brunch: 60F, BC; 110F, BC

scones served with pots of sweet butter and straw-berry jam. For lunch there is always an interesting array of seasonal salads and quiches, and on Sunday, filling brunches are offered. A bonus for many is the special nonsmoking section and the changing art ex-hibits that feature work by local artisans.

Verdeau–La Pomme de Terre Gourmande
25, passage Verdeau; access from 6, rue de la Grange Batelière (9th)

TELEPHONE
45-23-15-96

MÉTRO
Richelieu-Drouot, Montmartre

OPEN
Mon–Sat lunch only

CLOSED
Dinner; Sun; holidays; NAC

HOURS
Noon–3 P.M

RESERVATIONS
No

CREDIT CARDS
V

A LA CARTE
38–80F, BNC

PRIX FIXE
None

The French have had a love affair with the lowly potato for years. They serve it boiled, creamed, sautéed, and blended with garlic and Cantal cheese in the Auvergne dish *aligot*; and as everyone knows, *pommes frites* were the original french fries. With this in mind, it is easy to see why perfectly baked pota-toes, split in half and filled with everything imagin-able, have made Patrick and Yves Namura's two gour-met potato restaurants instant hits (see La Patata, page 53). If you can think of it, they have undoubt-edly put it on a potato and given it a name. La Forestière combines ham, mushrooms, and grated Gruyère in a béchamel sauce. The Bourguignonne is a potato topped with beef, carrots, and melted cheese and served with a side of fresh fruit. If you order the Rafting, you will have chopped chicken livers, Cantal cheese, shredded lettuce, corn, tomatoes, cucumbers, and herbs on your potato.

If none of the suggested combinations appeal, you can create your own dish from a long list of toppings. Most of the potatoes are served with a side salad, fresh fruit, and/or dessert. This all adds up to a real meal, and for fast food *à la française*, you can't beat it.

TENTH, ELEVENTH, TWELFTH, THIRTEENTH ARRONDISSEMENTS

These *quartiers populaires*, or traditional working-class neighborhoods of Paris, are not hives of tourist activity. They do, however, offer visitors an idea of how ordinary Parisians live their lives.

TENTH ARRONDISSEMENT

Many visitors to Paris pass through the tenth when they take a train from either the Gare du Nord or the Gare de l'Est. Another good reason to visit this part of Paris is to shop for china and crystal along Rue du Paradis, or to visit the Baccarat museum about halfway down the street.

TENTH ARRONDISSEMENT
Right Bank: Canal St-Martin, Place de la Republique, Rue du Paradis, Gare du Nord, and Gare de l'Est

TENTH ARRONDISSEMENT RESTAURANTS
Brasserie Flo

ELEVENTH AND TWELFTH ARRONDISSEMENTS

All that remains today of the Bastille, the infamous prison that was stormed during the French Revolution, is a faint outline traced on the cobblestones. *Vive le bicentennaire* for all the money that was infused into this once slummy area of Paris! The area around the new opera has been transformed into a mecca for new-wave hipsters, artists, nightclubs, and trendy restaurants and shops.

ELEVENTH AND TWELFTH ARRONDISSEMENTS
Right Bank: Bastille, New Opera at Bastille

ELEVENTH ARRONDISSEMENT RESTUARANTS

Jacques Mélac   La Vouivre
La Courtille   L'Écluse

THIRTEENTH ARRONDISSEMENT

Not much for the tourist here, except the beautiful tapestries at the Gobelins Factory, and a tour of Chinatown, where you can marvel that you *really* are in Paris, and not some city in the Far East.

THIRTEENTH ARRONDISSEMENT
Left Bank: Chinatown, Gare d'Austerlitz, Gobelins Tapestry Factory, Place d'Italie

Brasserie Flo
7, cour des Petites-Écuries (10th)

TELEPHONE
47-70-13-59
MÉTRO
Château d'Eau, Strasbourg-
St-Denis
OPEN
Daily lunch and dinner
CLOSED
Never; NAC
HOURS
Noon–3 P.M.,
dinner 7 P.M.–1 A.M.
RESERVATIONS
Necessary
CREDIT CARDS
AE, DC, MC, V
A LA CARTE
165–180F, BNC
PRIX FIXE
99F, 3 courses (no choices),
BC; 108F, *plat* and dessert, BC
(served from 11 P.M. on; several
choices for each course)

Brasserie Flo at 7, cour des Petites Écuries is not easy to find. The first time I went, I was sure the taxi driver was taking me on a wild goose chase, and when he left me off at the opening of a dark alley in a rather questionable neighborhood, I was sure of it. Once inside, however, the approach was completely forgotten. Seated along a banquette in one of the two long rooms with their dark wood walls, zinc bar, and waiters with long aprons serving a dressed-to-the-teeth crowd, you will truly feel you are in Paris.

Every day of the year Brasserie Flo is a great place to go for platters of oysters, Alsatian *choucroutes*—their specialty—onion soup, foie gras, and grilled meats. For late-nighters, a special menu is available from 11 P.M. until closing.

Jacques Mélac
42, rue Léon-Frot (11th)

TELEPHONE
43-70-59-27
MÉTRO
Charonne
OPEN
Mon–Fri bar, continuous
service (cold food), and lunch;
Tues and Thurs dinner
CLOSED
Mon, Wed, Fri dinner; Sat,
Sun; holidays; July 15–Aug 15
HOURS
9 A.M.–midnight, continuous
service; lunch noon–3:30 P.M.;
Tues and Thurs only, dinner
7:30–10:30 P.M.
RESERVATIONS
No
CREDIT CARDS
None
A LA CARTE
40–50F, BNC
PRIX FIXE
None

"If you want water, you must place your order the day before," states the handwritten sign hanging in this wine bar not far from the Bastille. Started by Jacques's father before World War II, Jacques Mélac is extremely popular, 100 percent authentic, and an absolute *must* for anyone who speaks even a little French and loves a good time. Jacques, with his handlebar mustache and infectious enthusiasm, broadcasts a message of welcome loud and clear to everyone who enters. Don't worry if your high-school French is a little rusty; after raising a few glasses at the bar with the rambunctious crowd, your French will improve dramatically. Go with a group or alone, and you are bound to be in good company, sampling several wines while munching on platters of *charcuterie* or Auvergne cheeses and loaves of chewy Poilâne bread. On Tuesday and Thursday nights, Jacques serves hot dishes and fantastic omelettes.

Winner of the 1981 Meilleur Pot, the wine bar also sells its own wine by the bottle or the case. This is the only wine bar in Paris boasting its own vineyard, with the vines growing on the roof and climbing up the outside walls. In September the grapes are harvested, and usually there is enough for a single barrel of wine, which is always cause for great celebration. Another cause is the annual arrival of Beaujolais *nouveau*, which all but flows in the street in mid-November, as do the patrons.

La Courtille
16, rue Guillaume Bertrand (11th)

One of my favorite finds for the last edition of *Cheap Eats in Paris* was Michel Monlau's La Courtille. A year or so ago he decided to sell the restaurant and open a boutique just a few blocks away (see note, below). Fortunately, the new owners of La Courtille, M. Pinson and M. Hillion, have continued Michel's tradition of serving good food at sensible prices, providing attentive service to a growing band of regulars and many, many *Cheap Eats* readers.

The best dining deal at both lunch and dinner is the prix fixe menu, which changes twice a year. With this list of eight *entrées*, *plats*, and desserts, no one ever goes away hungry or disappointed. In the winter, I like to start with the warm leek and smoked salmon *tarte*, then order either the fresh fish of the day or the *magret de canard* (duck breast) for the main course. I always make sure to save room for their dessert specialty, the *gâteau au chocolat amèricain*, a velvety chocolate cake surrounded by custard sauce.

Note: Michel Monlau's boutique, Baïkal, can be found at 15, Rue Lacharrière (11th). See *Cheap Sleeps in Paris*, page 184, for further details on this unique shop.

TELEPHONE
48-06-48-34

MÉTRO
St-Maur

OPEN
Mon–Fri lunch and dinner, Sat dinner only

CLOSED
Sat lunch, Sun; holidays; first 3 weeks in Aug

HOURS
Lunch noon–2 P.M., dinner 7:30–10:30 P.M.

RESERVATIONS
Advised for dinner

CREDIT CARDS
MC, V

A LA CARTE
160–170F, BNC

PRIX FIXE
Lunch: 70F, 3 courses, BNC; dinner 110F, BNC

La Vouivre
51, rue de Montreuil (11th)

"Where *are* you taking me?" my companion asked as we walked down a depressing street on our way to La Vouivre, a sensational *Cheap Eat* find in the wilds

TELEPHONE
43-70-28-27

MÉTRO
Nation, Faidherbe–Chaligny

OPEN
Tues–Fri lunch and dinner, Sat
dinner only

CLOSED
Sat lunch, Sun, Mon; holidays;
1 week in Aug

HOURS
Lunch noon–2 P.M., dinner
7:30–10 P.M.

RESERVATIONS
Advised

CREDIT CARDS
None

A LA CARTE
100F, BNC

PRIX FIXE
Lunch: 55F, 3 courses, (no
choices), BNC; lunch: 70F,
3 courses (some choices), BC;
dinner: 75F, 3 courses, BC
(served until 9 P.M. only)

of the 11th arrondissement. "You can't miss it," I assured him. You won't either, because it is the one bright spot on the entire street, with a green façade, red-geranium-filled window boxes, and lace curtains. Once inside the cheerful restaurant, with its yellow napkins and fresh flowers on each table, you will forget all about the approach and get down to the serious business of trying to decide what to eat. The menu provides a real tour de force of specialties from the Franche-Comté region in France, and the portions are served in sizes to please a stevedore.

Start with a pitcher of the drinkable house wine, and *pâté maison* spread on slices of dark country bread cut from the huge *pain de campagne* sitting on a table by the front door. The salads are almost meals in themselves, especially the hearts of artichoke spread with warm *chèvre*, and the *salade fleurie*, a beautiful mix of *crudités* arranged like a garden on a bed of greens. But, save room—there is much more to come: *raclette*, fondues, tender roast chicken, smoked sausages, fresh trout, and salmon in season. For dessert, order the custardy bread pudding or a dish of cool *sorbet*. From start to finish, you will have had a delicious meal and be very glad you made the safari to this non-touristy part of Paris.

L'Écluse (Bastille)
13, rue de la Roquette (11th)
Telephone: 48-05-19-12
Métro: Bastille

See page 42.

FOURTEENTH ARRONDISSEMENT

This artistic haven of the 1920s and 30s is now modernized and ugly, the victim of urban development without much taste.

The famous cafés—La Coupole, Le Select, Le Dôme, and La Rotunde—were the center of literary and artistic life in Paris between the two World Wars. This area was also home for dancer Isadora Duncan, and singer Edith Piaf performed often at the once-popular Bobino Music Hall.

FOURTEENTH ARRONDISSEMENT
Left Bank: Montparnasse

FOURTEENTH ARRONDISSEMENT RESTAURANTS

Batifol   Le Canard au Pot

Batifol
117 avenue du Général Leclerc (14th)
Telephone: 45-41-19-08
Métro: Alésia
Hours: 11 A.M.–1 A.M., continuous service

See page 35.

Le Canard au Pot
2, rue Boulard (14th)

You can expect unusually good food at Albertine and Michel's dignified restaurant. Located in an unlikely section of the untouristy 14th arrondissement, they serve specialties from the Landes region of France to an enthusiastic group of patrons. Once you've found it, as many readers have, you too will go back and will recommend it to others.

Ducks are the theme of the restaurant, and they are everywhere: in the form of planters, on the antique china and on the serving plates, and in the food you eat. You begin with duck soup or *fois gras de canard*. You then have a choice between *magret de canard à la moutarde* or *aux grains de cassis, confit de canard, steak de canard,* or, their specialty, *le canard*

TELEPHONE
43-22-79-62

MÉTRO
Denfert-Rochereau

OPEN
Thurs, Fri, Sun–Tues lunch and dinner; Sat dinner only

CLOSED
Wed lunch and dinner, Sat lunch; holidays; July

HOURS
Lunch 12:15–3 P.M., dinner 7:30–10 P.M.

RESERVATIONS
Advised

CREDIT CARDS
MC, V

A LA CARTE
175F, BNC
PRIX FIXE
None

au pot, a soul-warming duck stew with fresh vegetables. Other main dishes worth sampling are the veal kidneys in a delicate vinegar sauce and the *noisettes d'agneau au Roquefort* (lamb fillets in Roquefort sauce). While the desserts don't quite live up to the skill shown with the rest of the menu, the flaky fruit *tarte* flambéed with brandy is very nice.

FIFTEENTH ARRONDISSEMENT

A vast and generally untraveled region for most tourists, the 15th is basically a middle-class residential area signified by La Tour Montparnasse, the tallest building (and, by some standards, the ugliest) in Europe. In the 15th you will also find the Village Suisse, an expensive complex of antique shops selling everything imaginable at prices that are over the moon.

FIFTEENTH ARRONDISSEMENT
Left Bank: La Tour
Montparnasse

FIFTEENTH ARRONDISSEMENT RESTAURANTS

L'Amanguier
La Route du Beaujolais
Le Bistrot d'André

Le Café du Commerce
Le Petit Parnasse

L'Amanguier
46, boulevard Montparnasse (15th)
Telephone: 45-48-49-16
Métro: Falguière
  See page 53.

L'Amanguier
51, rue de Théâtre (15th)
Telephone: 45-77-04-01
Métro: Émile-Zola

  See page 53.

La Route du Beaujolais
17, rue de Lourmel (15th)

Reasonable prices and hearty food make La Route de Beaujolais worth a detour to this tourist-free corner of Paris, only a 15-minute walk from the Eiffel Tower. Sitting at wooden picnic tables under the glare of a stuffed bull doesn't quite make it the place to come for your first romantic dinner with a newly discovered love. It is worthy of consideration, however, if you enjoy the lively French art of dining well on the robust dishes that are now *à la mode* in Paris.

Order a pitcher of fruity Beaujolais to accompany

TELEPHONE
45-79-31-63
MÉTRO
Dupleix
OPEN
Mon–Fri lunch and dinner, Sat dinner only
CLOSED
Sat lunch, Sun; holidays; NAC
HOURS
Lunch noon–2:30 P.M., dinner 7–11 P.M.
RESERVATIONS
No

CREDIT CARDS
MC, V
A LA CARTE
125–140F, BNC
PRIX FIXE
Lunch: 90F, 3 courses, BNC

the *blanquette de veau*, coq au vin, or a brimming dish of roasted meat served with sautéed, mashed, fried, or scalloped potatoes. The desserts are good here, too, especially the chocolate mousse and the *tarte aux pommes*.

Le Bistrot d'André
232, rue Saint Charles (15th)

TELEPHONE
45-57-89-14
MÉTRO
Balard
OPEN
Mon–Fri lunch and dinner,
Sat dinner only
CLOSED
Sat lunch, Sun; holidays;
3 weeks in Aug
HOURS
Lunch noon–2 P.M.,
dinner 7:30–10 P.M.
RESERVATIONS
Advised, especially for lunch
CREDIT CARDS
V
A LA CARTE
110F, BNC
PRIX FIXE
Lunch only: 59F, 3 courses,
BNC

Hubert Gloaguen purchased this old, tired restaurant not too long ago and restored it to its original status as a canteen for the workers from the Citroën factory that used to dominate this arid corner of the 15th arrondissement. The simple, bright interior now honors automobile pioneer Andre Citröen with blow-ups of Citröen and his factory as it was in the old days. True, the bistro is far from the thick of things, but sometimes it is interesting to get away from all the tourist hoopla and see Paris from a Parisian's viewpoint.

The best time to come is at lunch, when the place is wall-to-wall with a good-looking *quartier* crowd sitting with their jackets off and their sleeves rolled up. The rushed service is efficient, considering the numbers of tables each waiter must serve. Another reason Cheap Eaters will want to make this a lunch stop is the 59F, three-course daily menu served in addition to an a la carte menu. A recent sampling included quiche Lorraine or fish *terrine* as an *entrée*, and *petit salé aux lentilles* or turkey with a *béarnaise* sauce for the *plat*. A choice of cheese or dessert, including picture-perfect fruit *tartes* and cakes, completes the courses. In the evening the scene is much calmer and there is no prix fixe menu, but the a la carte prices are reasonable and the food is always worth the safari.

Note: To avoid a long, dull Métro ride, take the No. 42 bus, which will drop you off across the street from the restaurant.

Le Café du Commerce
51, rue du Commerce (15th)

TELEPHONE
45-75-03-27

This once drab Cheap Eat has been lifted out of

the doldrums and transformed into a stylish two-level garden restaurant that is now the talk of the 15th. The eye-catching interior is set off by an open roof, masses of potted palms and just-picked flowers, and a sweeping staircase leading to balcony dining. Obvious care has been taken to retain the fin de siècle character of this former blue-collar soup kitchen. The numbered tables and chairs have been kept and so have the brass hat racks, ornate lamps, and mahogany serving station. The stern waiters continue to serve the same low-cost fare that has made Le Commerce a classic Cheap Eat for years. Even today, for around 90F, you can get a meal and a pitcher of the house wine. Pull out all the stops and order the more expensive items, and you'll have trouble topping 125F, wine included.

MÉTRO
Commerce, Émile-Zola

OPEN
Daily

CLOSED
Never; NAC

HOURS
Noon–midnight, continuous service

RESERVATIONS
No

CREDIT CARDS
AE, DC, MC, V

A LA CARTE
90–125F, BC

PRIX FIXE
None

Le Petit Parnasse
138, rue de Vaugirard (15th)

From the old photographs on the walls of Le Petit Parnasse you can see that not much has changed over the decades in this citadel of Cheap Eating near Montparnasse. In fact, some of the graying waiters and the guests sitting along the banquettes look as if they have been here for quite some time.

Don't expect any gourmet ruffles and flourishes with the food: although it is boarding school basic, it is still tasty and very French, and, above all, it is not going to upset many budgets.

The smart move for Cheap Eaters is to fill up on the prix fixe meals, order a pitcher of the house red or white wine, and be satisfied that you have had a decent meal without jeopardizing your children's educational funds.

TELEPHONE
47-83-29-52

MÉTRO
Falguière

OPEN
Mon–Fri lunch and dinner

CLOSED
Sat, Sun; holidays; 1st 3 weeks in Aug, last week in Dec

HOURS
Lunch noon–2:30 P.M., dinner 7–10 P.M.

RESERVATIONS
No

CREDIT CARDS
MC, V

A LA CARTE
140F, BNC

PRIX FIXE
73F, 3 courses, BNC; 97F, 3 courses, BNC

SIXTEENTH ARRONDISSEMENT

SIXTEENTH ARRONDISSEMENT
Right Bank: Avenue Foch, Bois de Boulogne, Jardin d'Acclimation, Marmottan Museum, Passy, Trocadéro

The 16th, along with the seventh, is one of Paris's toniest addresses, especially along Avenue Foch, where the real estate prices are geared to oil moguls and Arab sheiks. Elegant shopping can be found on Avenue Victor Hugo and Rue de Passy. The Trocadéro area, with its gardens, view of the Seine and Eiffel Tower, and complex of museums in the two wings of the Palais de Chaillot, forms the nucleus of tourist interest. At night the lighted fountains bring back the glamor of Art Deco Paris. Not to be overlooked is the Musée Marmottan, one of the hidden treasures of Parisian museums. Bequests and gifts have enriched the collection so much that it rivals that of the Musée d'Orsay in Impressionist art, especially the collection of Monets.

SIXTEENTH ARRONDISSEMENT

Au Clocher du Village   Musée du Vin

La Petite Tour   Restaurant des

Le Passé   Chauffeurs

Au Clocher du Village
8 bis, rue Verderet (16th)

TELEPHONE
42-88-35-87

MÉTRO
Église-Auteuil, exit Chardon Lagache

OPEN
Mon–Fri lunch and dinner

CLOSED
Sat, Sun; holidays; Aug; between Christmas and New Year's

HOURS
Lunch noon–2 P.M., dinner 7:30–10 P.M.

RESERVATIONS
Necessary

CREDIT CARDS
MC, V

A LA CARTE
185–195F, BNC

Wine presses and old baskets hang from beams; posters plaster the ceiling and walls; a shining copper samovar graces the bar; and enough trinkets and treasures to open a shop create a setting for provincial country dining at Au Clocher du Village. Reserve a table for a 9 P.M. dinner and you may be the only foreigner in the room. Admittedly it is close to nothing on the visitor's map, and the Métro ride is long for most, but trust me—it is worth the extra effort and time it takes to get here.

The food is prepared in the traditional fashion and served by a casually clad staff who banter back and forth with long-time customers. When ordering, stick with the daily specials or one of the grilled meats and avoid the *haricots verts* (green beans), and you will do fine. For starters, the mammoth plate of *crudités* or the artichoke hearts are a good bet. If you like apple tart, theirs is served warm with a tub of *crème fraîche* on the side to ladle over it.

PRIX FIXE
None

La Petite Tour
11, rue de la Tour (16th)

If only once during your stay in Paris you decide to have an exceptionally fine meal, you won't be disappointed by choosing Christiane and Freddy Israel's La Petite Tour in the Passy district of the 16th arrondissement. Offering marvelous food, correct service, and a quiet ambience, an evening here is a dining pleasure you will remember long after leaving Paris. The food, a blend of classic French with modern overtones, relies on first-class products, precise preparation, and elegant presentation.

If you visit in the fall, order the masterfully cooked wild game. One of the most outstanding dishes is a robust venison stew with whole baby vegetables. It is almost impossible to list all the other specialties, as the menu is long and changes with market availability and the seasons. Always on the menu is the delicate lobster bisque and the *filets de sole aux mandarines*. The *caneton aux pêches* (duckling with peaches) is delicious and so is the simple *fricassée de poulet au vinaigre* (stewed chicken in a vinegar sauce). You simply must save room for one of the picture-perfect desserts, especially the *pêches Pantagruel* or the blissfully light *île flottante* (floating island).

Of course all this does not fall into the budget category, but while sipping an after-dinner Cognac, I am sure you will agree with the many others who have been here before you that the elegant meal has been well worth the higher tab.

TELEPHONE
45-20-09-31, 45-20-09-97
MÉTRO
Passy (lots of steps; a taxi is better)
OPEN
Mon–Sat lunch and dinner
CLOSED
Sun; holidays; Aug
HOURS
Lunch noon–2:30 P.M., dinner 7:30–10:30 P.M.
RESERVATIONS
Essential
CREDIT CARDS
AE, DC, MC, V
A LA CARTE
325–350F, BNC
PRIX FIXE
None

Le Passé
6, rue Pergolèse (16th)

Straightforward country cooking has been the forte for years at Le Passé, the type of bare-bones

TELEPHONE
45-00-56-30

MÉTRO
Pte Dauphine
OPEN
Mon–Fri lunch and dinner,
Sat dinner only
CLOSED
Sat lunch, Sun; holidays;
2 weeks in Aug
HOURS
Lunch noon–2:30 P.M.,
dinner 7:30–10:30 P.M.
RESERVATIONS
No
CREDIT CARDS
MC, V
A LA CARTE
100–120F, BNC
PRIX FIXE
Lunch 65F, 3 set courses, BC

little restaurant most Paris neighborhoods are full of and visitors never find.

It is a rumpled spot, where the seats are worn shiny and smooth by years of use by patrons who know each other and most of each other's business as well. The friendly owner, M. Atassi, shuffles between tables, serving, chatting, and making certain everyone is happy.

The standard menu of salads, meats, and desserts provides the faithful with honest, no-frills fare at prices that are refreshingly low for this posh pocket of the 16th arrondissement.

Musée du Vin
5–7, Square Charles Dickens, top of rue des Eaux (16th)

TELEPHONE
45-25-63-26
MÉTRO
Passy
OPEN
Daily lunch and wine tasting
CLOSED
Major holidays; NAC
HOURS
Restaurant: noon–3 P.M. for
lunch and wine tasting,
museum: 2–6 P.M.
RESERVATIONS
No
CREDIT CARDS
AE, DC, MC, V
A LA CARTE
45–80F, BNC
PRIX FIXE
Lunch only: 99F (*plat*, dessert
or cheese, coffee or tea)

If you are a wine buff, a visit to the Musée du Vin is an interesting way to spend an hour or two in Paris. Buried in a part of Passy few tourists ever see, the museum is surrounded by beautiful apartment buildings designed by Freimet, who has many examples of his work displayed at the Musée d'Orsay. The best way to visit is to arrive about 1 P.M., have a light lunch in the restaurant, sample a glass or two of a special vintage, and then wander through the *caves*, which display almost every aspect of wine growing and production in France.

There is a wine boutique selling good-quality *grande marque* wines directly from the vineyards. Prices aren't in the bargain-basement category, but they are very reasonable when you consider the quality of the wine.

Restaurant des Chauffeurs
8, Chausée de la Muette (16th)

TELEPHONE
42-88-50-05
MÉTRO
La Muette

If you want to experience the type of family-run operation that seems to be on its way out in today's Paris, you will find a good example at Restaurant des Chauffeurs.

The restaurant has been collecting anecdotes and acquiring patina for years, and it is easy to imagine that the hardcore regulars leaning against the bar have been here for years as well. You will see another group of habitués at the outside tables, idling away the afternoon examining what upscale Parisians who frequent Passy are wearing *this* year.

The almost-readable, purple-inked menu features trucker-sized portions of French comfort food. A typical selection might include a bowl of vegetable soup, *pâté*, or herring, followed by sole *meunière* with steamed potatoes, pork with noodles, or, the specialty, liver with bacon and tomatoes. The desserts are simple versions of *clafoutis*, rice pudding, and fruit *tartes*. With a pitcher of house wine, a 100 francs will see you out the door.

OPEN
Daily

CLOSED
Christmas day; January 1; May 1; Easter; Aug 15–25

HOURS
Noon–10 P.M., continuous service

RESERVATIONS
No

CREDIT CARDS
V

A LA CARTE
100F, BC

PRIX FIXE
54F, 3 courses, BNC

SEVENTEENTH ARRONDISSEMENT

Basically this is an upscale residential area that includes the Palais des Congrès (a convention center with restaurants), several movie theaters, and the first stop in Paris for the Charles de Gaulle airport bus.

SEVENTEENTH ARRONDISSEMENT
RESTAURANTS

Chez Fred	La Petite Auberge
Chocolat Viennois	Le Petit Salé
Joy in Food	Le Relais de Venise
La Bonne Cuisine	L'Étoile Verte
L'Amanguier	

Chez Fred
190 bis, boulevard Péreire (17th)

TELEPHONE
45-74-20-48

MÉTRO
Péreire, Pte Maillot

OPEN
Mon–Fri lunch and dinner,
Sat dinner only

CLOSED
Sat lunch, Sun; holidays; Aug

HOURS
Lunch 12:30–2 P.M.,
dinner 7–10:30 P.M.

RESERVATIONS
Yes

CREDIT CARDS
AE, DC, MC, V

A LA CARTE
200–220F, BC

PRIX FIXE
Lunch: 150F, 3 courses, BC

When food awards are handed out, Chez Fred is always a winner. It is a friendly spot, known to its many fans for its value and for bistro-style cooking that is made to be eaten, not looked at. The inside is 1930s grand-mère, with beveled mirrors, old pieces of china on display, a hanging collection of umbrellas, and Fred's overweight dog, who is usually lying by the entrance. Fred, the person responsible for all of this, wears an authentic sheriff's badge just in case anyone wants to question his authority. He presides over every table, suggesting certain dishes or appropriate combinations. He speaks English, as do most of his waiters (with varying degrees of success).

At the entrance, a big table overflows with first-course temptations: marinated mushrooms, herring, pâtés, *terrines*, and assorted salads. The plat du jour promises lamb on Monday, *petit salé* on Tuesday, and *tête de veau* on Wednesday. Thursday is pot-au-feu, Friday *boeuf à la mode*, and Saturday lamb again. In addition, there is a full range of Lyonnaise offerings, truly wonderful if you love *saucisse* (sausage) and *andouilette*. This is the place to ignore your diet and indulge in dessert. The chocolate cake with rich dark chocolate frosting is worth dieting for a week, as is the *crème brûlée*.

Chocolat Viennois
118, rue des Dames (17th)

If you are strolling along the colorful Rue de Levis shopping street, this is a good place to stop in for a quick cup of chocolate topped with whipped cream, a nice afternoon pastry, or a full-blown lunch or dinner. The wood-paneled interior of this cozy restaurant resembles a mountain chalet. There are several seating areas in the tiny main room. Tables are tucked into corners, and special tables are reserved for nonsmokers—a real plus. If you see something you like chances are it is for sale, from the painted wooden fruit and the flower arrangements to the chocolate and sugar tins on display everywhere. The lineup of taste temptations ranges from huge salads, *raclette*, fondue, and quiches to savory *tartes* and meat-based dishes. Desserts such as apple strudel, fruit crumble with cream, and an almost illegally rich chocolate cake served with vanilla ice cream and chocolate sauce will destroy every ounce of willpower a dieter can muster.

TELEPHONE
42-93-34-40

MÉTRO
Villiers

OPEN
Mon–Sat

CLOSED
Sat dinner, Sun; holidays; NAC

HOURS
Lunch noon–3 P.M., tea 3–7 P.M., dinner 7–10 P.M.

RESERVATIONS
Advised for lunch

CREDIT CARDS
AE, DC, MC, V

A LA CARTE
40–80F, BNC

PRIX FIXE
None

Joy in Food
2, rue Truffaut, corner of rue des Dames and rue Truffaut (17th)

If you think *vegetarian* means only lentils and brown rice, you haven't had a meal at Joy in Food. I found it one day while just walking by. The clean whitewashed interior and tempting aromas beckoned me, and I had to try it. I am glad I did. The light, imaginative vegetarian cuisine, and a final bill that matched the size of this tiny restaurant, made it a super Cheap Eat surprise.

The young owner, Guillamme Botté, puts on a virtual one-person show as he cooks and serves from his compact kitchen in full view of everyone. The room capacity is 16, and by 12:30 or 1:00, all seats

TELEPHONE
43-87-96-79

MÉTRO
Rome, Place de Chichy

OPEN
Mon–Sat lunch and dinner; Tues, Fri, Sat dinner only

CLOSED
Mon, Wed, Thur, Sun; Aug

HOURS
Lunch 12:30–3 P.M., dinner 7:30–10 P.M.

RESERVATIONS
No

are taken by some of the growing number of diners who have come to appreciate Botté's health-conscious meals and no-smoking policy. Every day they can depend on having a savory *tarte*, a plat du jour, or one of several omelettes as a main course. Assorted *crudités*, crisp salads, vegetable pâté, and baked *chèvre* on toast are the tempting starters. Even hard-core dieters succumb to the *gâteau aux poires*, (a dense pear cake), and the apple crumble topped with *crème fraîche*. No wine is served, but who cares? Fresh carrot juice, banana milkshakes, and herbal teas more than make up for it. Located in a tourist wilderness in a corner of the 17th, Joy in Food is definitely worth a visit, whether or not you are a vegetarian.

La Bonne Cuisine
17, rue Biot (17th)

In Pigalle it is almost impossible to eat anywhere that isn't geared to raucous tourists. Although La Bonne Cuisine is only a few blocks from this distressingly seedy part of Paris, it is a classic example of a comfortable, slightly middle-aged *restaurant du quartier*. The locals are out in full force and arrive with huge appetites to fill up on *la cuisine faite par le patron*, Jacky Loize. For more than 10 years at this location, M. Loize has been feeding his friends and neighbors with a lineup of solid fare that includes all the standards. Here you can select from a long menu that highlights pâtés, *terrines*, pork sausage in white wine, leg of lamb, steak *tartare*, *entrecôte*, and a long list of daily specials. While not an address to remember if you are a serious gourmet with only one day to spend eating in Paris, it is one to remember if you are near Pigalle and looking for a well-priced spot with good food that the locals thrive on.

L'Amanguier
43, avenue des Ternes (17th)
Telephone: 43-80-19-28
Métro: Ternes

See page 53.

CREDIT CARDS
None
A LA CARTE
45–65F, BC
PRIX FIXE
None

TELEPHONE
45-22-54-35
MÉTRO
Place de Clichy
OPEN
Mon–Fri lunch and dinner, Sat dinner only
CLOSED
Sat lunch, Sun; 8 days in Feb; most holidays; Aug
HOURS
Lunch noon–2 P.M., dinner 7–9:45 P.M.
RESERVATIONS
Necessary
CREDIT CARDS
AE, DC, MC, V
A LA CARTE
150F, BNC
PRIX FIXE
Lunch: 65F, 3 courses, BNC, dinner 80F, 3 courses, BNC

La Petite Auberge
38, rue Laugier (17th)

For superb dining in the finest French tradition, reserve a table for lunch or dinner at La Petite Auberge. Longtime owner and chef Leo Harbonnier has retired and turned over the culinary reigns to the talented Joël Ducloux and his charming wife Jackie, who acts as the hostess. In the transition, I am happy to report that La Petite Auberge is better than ever! The best dishes of M. Harbonnier have been kept, and Joël has added many of his own signature recipes. The polite service fulfills the expectations of the most discriminating patron, paying attention to the little details that make such a difference.

No matter what you order, you will be pleased. Star *entrées* are the *ravioles d'escargots au beurre de Roquefort* (ravioli stuffed with snails) and the *charlotte de lotte* (lotte in puff pastry). Top main courses include M. Harbonnier's famous turbot in a mushroom cream sauce, and tender pink lamb. When you are seated you will be asked if you want the hot lemon soufflé for dessert. Yes, you do! At least one of you does. the light and flaky *mille feuilles*—puff pastry Napoléons—are without question the best in Paris, so it is always a difficult decision.

La Petite Auberge, as always, is a good choice for a Last Night or special celebration meal.

TELEPHONE
47-63-85-51, 47-63-85-81

MÉTRO
Ternes, Pereire

OPEN
Tues–Sat lunch and dinner, Sun lunch only

CLOSED
Sun dinner, Mon; holidays; Aug

HOURS
Lunch noon–3 P.M., dinner 7–11 P.M.

RESERVATIONS
Yes

CREDIT CARDS
MC, V

A LA CARTE
Lunch: 275F, BNC; dinner: 300F, BNC

PRIX FIXE
160F, 3 courses, BNC

Le Petit Salé
99, avenue des Ternes (17th)

Warning: This is *not* an affair for the timid eater!

At this little Cheap Eat hideaway, where heaping plates, good fellowship, and crowded tables are the call of the day, the substantial specialty is *petit salé*: salt pork cooked with vegetables and lentils and served with a big basket of crusty bread to mop up the wonderful juices.

If salt pork isn't your passion, there is a handful of other choices: house *terrines, cassoulet,* steak, leg of lamb, liver, and, in summer, cold meats, attractive

TELEPHONE
45-74-10-57

MÉTRO
Ternes

OPEN
Mon–Sat bar (continuous service), lunch, and dinner

CLOSED
Sun; most holidays; NAC

HOURS
Bar noon–11 P.M., continuous service; lunch noon–3 P.M.; dinner 7–11 P.M.

salads, and light desserts. Le Petit Salé always has a good cheese selection from the famous Ferme St-Honoré. Wine is charged according to how much you consume.

Lunchtime, especially in the winter, can be a madhouse, so schedule your arrival accordingly.

Le Relais de Venise
271, boulevard Péreire (17th)

It is on every Parisian's Cheap Eat map, and it should be on yours. You can't call for reservations because they do not take them. As a result, you must go early or very late, because there is almost always a line waiting outside the Relais de Venise, better known as l'Entrecôte. Their long-standing formula for success has been widely imitated, but never improved on. Here is the deal: for 86F, you will be served a salad and an *entrecôte* steak with *pommes frites*. Desserts designed to make Betty Crocker drool are extra and so is wine. All this is served to an appreciative audience in a cheerful room with a mural of the Grand Canal in Venice along one side and tables draped in multicolored cloths.

L'Étoile Verte
13, rue Brey (17th)

For years L'Étoile Verte has been known as a near miracle in Cheap Eating. This plain Jane restaurant not far from the Arc de Triomphe and the Champs-Élysées is a good one to remember, because it is open 365 days a year. The atmosphere and decor match the food: basic. The food is dispensed with dispatch and unfailing good humor to an international set of Cheat Eaters and neighbors who love a bargain. The a la carte menu goes on forever, listing more than enough choices to please everyone, from your picky five-year-old to Aunt Sally on a diet. In addition there are daily blue-plate specials, and a prix fixe menu that is positively astonishing when you consider it includes three courses, all with four or five selections that change daily, *and* wine.

EIGHTEENTH ARRONDISSEMENT

Montmartre captivates visitors with its picturesque winding streets, magnificent views of Paris from the steps of Sacré Coeur, and its history as the heart and soul of artistic Paris at the turn of the century, when the Moulin Rouge and Toulouse-Lautrec were at their peak. Today, Montmartre is more like a village, slightly removed from the normal hustle and bustle of Paris. It is also a study in contrasts, as nostalgia mixes with the crass commercialism of Pigalle and the Place du Tertre, a mecca for tourists and third-rate artists hawking their dubious wares.

EIGHTEENTH ARRONDISSEMENT
Right Bank: Montmartre, Sacré Coeur

EIGHTEENTH ARRONDISSEMENT RESTAURANTS

Au Pierrot de la Butte	Lionel
Chez Francis	Rendez-vous des Chauf-
Gueule et Gosier	feurs
La Casserole	Restaurant le Petit Chose
Le Maquis	Restaurant Marie-Louise

Au Pierrot de la Butte
41, rue Caulaincourt (18th)

Au Pierrot de la Butte is a good restaurant that keeps getting better. Many places in Montmartre and the surrounding area are overrated, overpriced, and overcrowded. Not this one. It is a little spot, not intended for the tourist crowd, but rather for the neighborhood French and others in "the know" who enjoy dignified dining at reasonable prices. The nicest table is the one by the back window, which overlooks the garden below.

In addition to the prix fixe, there is a well-selected a la carte list. I like to start with the *salade landaise* (green salad with mushrooms and smoked duck) or the *oeufs du Pierrot* (poached eggs with béarnaise sauce), and follow that with a grilled steak or the plat du jour. For dessert, the crème caramel or the chocolate mousse are the top favorites.

TELEPHONE
46-06-06-97

MÉTRO
Lamarck-Caulaincourt

OPEN
Mon–Sat lunch and dinner

CLOSED
Sun; major holidays; NAC

HOURS
Lunch noon–2 P.M., dinner 7:30–11 P.M.

RESERVATIONS
Advised for weekend evenings

CREDIT CARDS
MC, V

A LA CARTE
175F, BNC

PRIX FIXE
Lunch and dinner until 10 P.M.: 100F, 3 courses, BNC

Note: The restaurant may be closed for lunch in the future. Call ahead to make sure before you go.

Chez Francis
122, rue Caulaincourt (18th)

TELEPHONE
42-64-60-62

MÉTRO
Lamarck-Caulaincourt (No. 80 bus stops across street)

OPEN
Thur–Mon lunch and dinner, Wed dinner only

CLOSED
Tues, Wed lunch; holidays; October 1–8; NAC

HOURS
Lunch noon–2:30 P.M., dinner 7–10:30 P.M.

RESERVATIONS
For Sun lunch

CREDIT CARDS
AE, V

A LA CARTE
180F, BNC

PRIX FIXE
110F, 3 courses, BNC

Chez Francis is the type of restaurant I could come to every day and feel at home. Overseen by hard-working owner Felicité Erguy, its mood is perfect old-fashioned Paris: a bustling and cramped dining room with varnished paint, yellowing walls, smoky mirrors, and interesting Montmartre habitués sitting at their regular tables. On Sundays the restaurant is alive with high-spirited family groups lingering on the covered terrace over a leisurely three-hour lunch. The rich southwestern-inspired cuisine is from the old school that pays no attention to calorie watching. Serious followers of this type of cooking will adore the wide selection on the prix fixe menu. First-rate *entrées* include *terrine de Périgord, jambon de Bayonne,* and *salade landaise* filled with chunks of foie gras. The specialty is paella and simply not to be missed if it is one of your favorites. Other top choices are the leg of lamb, *confit de porc,* and *escalope de veau aux pleurottes et crème* (veal with mushrooms and cream). After a sumptuous meal it is hard to contemplate dessert, but if you can, try the *oeufs à la neige* or the *gâteau basque.* Later on, wander back up the hill to the top of Montmartre, stand on the steps of Sacré-Coeur, and gaze over all of Paris lying at your feet. It is an experience you won't soon forget—I guarantee it.

Gueule et Gosier
6, rue Aristide-Bruant (18th)

TELEPHONE
42-23-70-83

MÉTRO
Abbesses

OPEN
Tues–Sat dinner only

Montmartre is overflowing with tourists and tourist traps of every type, making the pursuit of decent gastronomical pleasures without astronomical tabs more and more difficult. But don't despair; take heart. Tucked away on a little side street near the Métro Abbesses is this special dining find that has escaped all the tourist hoopla of the *quartier*. Open only for dinner, M. and Mme Marchand's cozy restaurant serving the food of the Périgord region of France has attracted a loyal food-loving clientele of local residents. A meal here will undoubtedly be romantic, memorable, and reasonable, in addition to pleasing the palate.

Gueule et Gosier means, colloquially, "good food and good drink." You will have both here if you order *only* from the prix fixe menu and select the chef's specialties. Great care and attention is given to the preparation of these dishes, and they are served by Mme Marchand with pride. The portions are hefty, so start with one of the first-rate salads of crunchy leaf lettuce, arugula, and *chèvre*. Move on to the meaty *cassoulet quercynois*: a *confit* of duck, pork, and sausage with beans, tomatoes, and a *gratinée* topping. The desserts, unfortunately, are forgettable, but if you insist, a *sorbet* is a light ending.

CLOSED
Lunch; Sun, Mon; holidays; Aug

HOURS
Dinner 7–10 P.M.

RESERVATIONS
Advised

CREDIT CARDS
MC, V

A LA CARTE
180F, BNC

PRIX FIXE
95F, 4 courses, BNC

La Casserole
17, rue Boinod (18th)

For a dining experience in an atmosphere found nowhere else on this planet, head for La Casserole. Located on the backside of Montmartre, the restaurant consists of several rooms festooned with an endless assortment of knickknacks, stuffed animals, plants, doo-dads, fishnets, seashells, cooing birds, pots, pans, feathers, fans, flags, banners, and badges, all hung on the beams, ceilings, and walls, and in the windows and over the doors. No space has been left unadorned—including the unisex toilet, which you absolutely *must* see to believe.

But what about the food and the service? They are great. The portions are copious, the service friendly, and the diners fun to watch and be with. In the fall and winter, all sorts of wild game heads the list of favorite dishes to order. During the rest of the year, traditional preparations of robust French standards keep everyone well fed and happy. Look for goose,

TELEPHONE
42-54-50-97

MÉTRO
Simplon, Marcadet-Poissonniers

OPEN
Tues–Sat lunch and dinner

CLOSED
Sun, Mon; holidays; Aug

HOURS
Lunch noon–2 P.M., dinner 7:30–10:30 P.M.

RESERVATIONS
Necessary

CREDIT CARDS
MC, V

A LA CARTE
140F, BNC

PRIX FIXE
90F, 3 courses (limited selections), BNC

pigeon, chicken, duck, and grilled steak, all garnished with large servings of potatoes. The desserts are basic, but made here and recommended, especially the chocolate mousse, and the homemade nougat ice cream with a honey, orange, and caramel topping.

Le Maquis
69, rue Caulaincourt (18th)

TELEPHONE
42-59-76-07
MÉTRO
Lamarck-Caulaincourt
OPEN
Mon–Sat lunch and dinner
CLOSED
Sun; major holidays; NAC
HOURS
Lunch noon–2 P.M.,
dinner 8–10 P.M.
RESERVATIONS
Yes
CREDIT CARDS
MC, V
A LA CARTE
165F, BNC
PRIX FIXE
Lunch: 70F, 2 courses (2 *entrée* choices, 1 *plat*), BC

Montmartre is full of greasy spoons dedicated to scooping in the tourists, and in the process, turning off the locals. Well protected from this dining circus is Le Maquis, one of the increasingly hard-to-find *restaurants de quartier* with a loyal following for its sound food served at a consistently fair price. The 55-seat dining room is rather formal, with potted palms, fresh flowers, pink linen tablecloths, and waiters clad in black. In the summer the tiny terrace along the front is a good vantage point for the Parisian pastime of people-watching.

The seasonal menu is dedicated to traditional specialties, beautifully prepared from the best ingredients. The *carte* changes four times a year and the prix fixe lunch menu every day, so it's virtually impossible to describe all the possibilities. If I'm here in the spring, I look for the warm turnips in a bacon dressing or the fresh asparagus vinaigrette as an *entrée*. For the main dish, I hope to find the succulent rabbit in a tart mustard sauce or the leg of lamb with its trio of fresh vegetables. The desserts are all *à la maison* and may include a delicate orange mousse with a hot chocolate sauce or a flaming *crème brûlée*.

Lionel
26, rue Yvonne-le-Tac (18th)

TELEPHONE
46-06-20-51
MÉTRO
Abbesses
OPEN
Mon–Sat lunch and dinner

Lionel is one of Paris's best-kept dining secrets. Small, intimate, and truly special, it is on a quiet street in Montmartre just off the Place des Abbesses. The tiny, romantic room, which seats 23, has tables set with gleaming china and crystal, fresh flowers, and candles at night. It is the perfect choice for dinner with a new or old love, especially if you arrive about 9 P.M. and ask for a window table.

The menus change ever so often and feature seasonal and personal specialties of the chef. Be sure to ask what the *idée du jour* is, because it usually reflects the best he has to offer. In the spring, *entrée* winners are the flaky pastry leaves filled with *chèvre*; the fragrant, garlicky Mediterranean fish-based soup with a basket of crunchy croutons; or the fresh haddock marinated in green peppers. For the main course, try the smoked salmon and fresh pasta sprinkled with chopped chives, or, for a change of pace, the tender calf's liver in a honey and vinegar sauce. The desserts are very seductive, but not heavy, especially the double chocolate mousse, and the popular *oeufs à la neige*.

CLOSED
Sun; holidays; Aug

HOURS
Lunch noon–2 P.M., dinner 7–11 P.M.

RESERVATIONS
Yes

CREDIT CARDS
MC, V

A LA CARTE
210F, BNC

PRIX FIXE
Lunch: 80F, 3 courses, BNC; dinner: 140F, 3 courses, BNC

Rendez-vous des Chauffeurs
11, rue des Portes Blanches (18th)

If you are willing to go where other tourists fear to tread, want a lot for less, and are willing to pay cash, you should go to the Rendez-vous des Chauffeurs. This nostalgic throwback to the past is an honest-to-goodness neighborhood hangout where the decor has been given a minimum of attention and importance. *Nouvelle cuisine* never caught on here, and the food doesn't aspire to the gourmet level, but the restaurant is always packed with a comfortable clientele eager to lap up the adored staples of bourgeoise cooking. Owner Roger Lafarge and his wife Étiennette have been here for 25 years, cooking, serving, and caring for patrons: mostly pensioners, widowers, and sweet neighborhood couples who eat here on a daily basis. The bargain du jour is definitely the 48F, three-course meal, which includes wine. Starting with a plate of fresh *crudités* and continuing on to the *plat* garnished with fresh produce from the Lafarge farm in Turenne, down to the last drop of the homemade *patisserie*, a meal here is a filling and very satisfying one that any Cheap Eater in Paris will appreciate.

TELEPHONE
42-64-04-17

MÉTRO
Marcadet-Poissonniers

OPEN
Fri–Tues lunch and dinner

CLOSED
Wed, Thur; holidays; July and Aug

HOURS
Lunch noon–2:30 P.M., dinner 7–10 P.M.

RESERVATIONS
No

CREDIT CARDS
None

A LA CARTE
75F, BNC

PRIX FIXE
48F, 3 courses, BC (not available Sun)

Restaurant le Petit Chose
41, rue des Trois Frères (18th)

TELEPHONE
42-64-49-15

MÉTRO
Abbesses

OPEN
Daily lunch and dinner

CLOSED
Never; NAC

HOURS
Lunch noon–2 P.M.,
dinner 8–11 P.M.

RESERVATIONS
Essential for dinner and
weekends

CREDIT CARDS
AE, MC, V

A LA CARTE
175F, BNC

PRIX FIXE
Mon–Fri lunch only: 55F, 3
courses (no choices), BNC;
89F, 3 courses, BNC; 140F,
4 courses, BNC

"We're going to take you to our favorite small Montmartre restaurant—it has atmosphere, out-of-the-ordinary cooking, reasonable prices, and you won't see another tourist all night," said my friends who live in Paris. Impossible, I thought. But no, not at Le Petit Chose, owned by Jean-Marc Drumel. This wonderful find seats only 31 people in a main-floor dining area with a little mezzanine above it. Linen napkins, silver candle-sticks, fresh flowers, and memorabilia of the poet Rimbaud all work nicely together to create a very intimate *montmartois* mood.

Service is laid-back, even slow at times, and not every dish inspires rave reviews. But in the course of a meal there are many pleasant surprises, such as the *salade de crottin chaud déguisé* (two pieces of *chèvre* surrounded by tomatoes, fresh mint sprigs, quail eggs, almonds, and pieces of apple) and the escargot stew (a ragout of snails with zucchini, tomatoes, and *cèpes*, seasoned with fresh dill). If lamb is offered, order it—it is tender, moist, and perfectly cooked in a creamy garlic sauce. The *confit de canard* (preserved duck) left something to be desired, but not the grilled trout or the beef fillet with a mustard glaze. The desserts, which lean heavily toward chocolate, are a perfect ending to a large meal, especially the *soufflé au chocolate*, and the *gâteau chocolate menthe* (chocolate cake flavored with crème de menthe).

Restaurant Marie-Louise
5, rue Championnet (18th)

TELEPHONE
46-06-85-55

MÉTRO
Simplon

OPEN
Tues–Sat lunch and dinner

CLOSED
Sun, Mon; holidays; Aug

Most people pass hurriedly through this part of Paris on their way to the flea market at Clignancourt. In so doing, they are missing a restaurant that has been serving wonderful food for three decades.

From the street it looks like a thousand others and probably would not catch your attention unless you knew about it. Inside, the two rooms are very *correct*, as the French say, with thick white linens, shining crystal, fresh flowers, and a clientele that is as hearty as the food. Marie-Louise is the sort of restaurant where you must arrive hungry to best appreciate the beautifully cooked servings of classical French cooking.

Planning your meal requires a certain amount of careful thought, because owner and chef Jean Coillot does not believe in letting anyone go away hungry, and the portions are large. You might start with the *salade maison,* a mixture of finely sliced ham, mushrooms, celery, and lettuce in a light cream dressing. The *pâté maison* or the *rosette* (a pork sausage served in slices) also makes a good beginning. The house specialty, *poularde Marie-Louise* (a classic version of chicken seasoned with paprika) and the *rognons de veau Madère* (veal kidneys in Madeira wine sauce) are comforting main dishes. After a seasonal dessert or the chocolate mousse, you will have happily finished a fine French meal that will be a special memory of Paris.

HOURS
Lunch noon–2 P.M., dinner 7:30–10 P.M.

RESERVATIONS
Yes

CREDIT CARDS
DC, V

A LA CARTE
150–165F, BNC

PRIX FIXE
100F, 3 courses, BNC

UNIVERSITY RESTAURANTS

Institutional food, even in Paris, is nothing to write home about, but it *is* cheap. CROUS is a chain of university restaurants that offers so-so food at unbeatable prices. Anyone can buy tickets at any CROUS restaurant, but if you have a student card, the price will be even lower. For nonstudents, prices start around 28F per meal. Both students and nonstudents can save more money by buying a book of ten meal tickets. All restaurants generally serve lunch from 11:30 A.M. to 1 P.M. and dinner from 6 to 8 P.M., Monday through Friday, but it always pays to check before you go, because hours change. On weekends and in the summer, openings rotate, so check the CROUS schedule to see which ones are operating. Warning: The lines can be discouraging.

The following list of CROS restaurants includes those that are most convenient, so it is by no means exhaustive. For a complete list of all the CROUS university restaurants in Paris and their hours of operation, go to CROUS, 39, avenue Georges Bernanos (5th), 40-51-36-00, Métro Port-Royal.

CROUS RESTAURANTS IN PARIS

Bullier, 39, avenue Georges Bernanos (5th) Métro: Port-Royal

Censier, 31, rue Geoffroy St-Hilaire (5th) Métro: Censier-Daubenton

Chatelet, 10, rue Jean Calvin (5th) Métro: Censier-Daubenton

Cuvier-Jussieu, 8 bis, rue Cuvier (5th) Métro: Jussieu

Assas, 92, rue d'Assas (6th) Métro: Notre-Dame-des-Champs

Mabillon, 3, rue Mabillon (6th) Métro: Mabillon

Mazet, 5, rue Mazet (6th) Métro: Odéon

Grand Palais, Cours la Reine (8th) Métro: Champs-Élysées

Citeaux, 45, boulevard Diderot (12th) Métro: Gare de Lyon

Dareau, 13–17, rue Dareau (14th) Métro: St-Jacques

Chu Necker, 156, rue de Vaugirard (15th) Métro: Pasteur

I.U.T., 143, avenue de Versailles (16th) Métro: Chardon-Lagache

QUICK REFERENCE LIST

This Quick Reference List contains the restaurants that fall into the Big Splurge category, those offering continuous food service, those open on Sunday, and those open in August.

BIG SPLURGE

These restaurants are more expensive, but because they offer such fine cuisine, good service, and overall value, they are included for those with more flexible budgets.

À la Tour Montlhéry (Chez Denise) (1st)	34
Bofinger (4th)	62
Chez Julien (4th)	64
La Fermette Marbeuf 1900 (8th)	114
La Marlotte (6th)	90
L'Ambassade d'Auvergne (3rd)	58
La Petite Auberge (17th)	141
La Petite Tour (16th)	135
Le Berthoud (5th)	78
L'Écaille de P.C.B. (6th)	92
Le Soufflé (1st)	45
L'Excuse (4th)	67
Lionel (18th)	146
l'Oulette (4th)	68
Mossonnier (5th)	82
Restaurant Chez Marius (5th)	83

RESTAURANTS OFFERING CONTINUOUS FOOD SERVICE

À la Cour de Rohan (6)   84
Tues–Fri and Sun, noon–7:30 P.M., Sat noon–11:30 P.M.

À la Tour de Montlhéry (Chez Denise) (1)   34
Mon–Sat 6 A.M.–7 P.M., non-stop

American Pershing Hall (8)   111
Daily 8:30 A.M.–midnight

Au Chien Qui Fume (1)   35
Daily noon–2 A.M.

Au Petit Fer à Cheval (4)   62
Daily noon–midnight

Batifol (1, 3, 14)   35, 57, 129
Daily 11 A.M.–1 A.M.

Brasserie Balzar (5)   74
Daily 8 A.M.–1 A.M.

Brasserie de l'Île St-Louis (4)   63
Fri–Tues 11:30 A.M.–2 A.M.

Brasserie Ma Bourgogne (4)   63
Daily 8 A.M.–2 A.M.

Chez Jenny (3)   64
Daily 11:30 A.M.–1 A.M.

Chicago Meatpackers (1)   36
Daily 11:30 A.M.–1 A.M.

Chocolat Viennois (17)   139
Mon–Sat Lunch noon–3 P.M., tea 3–7 P.M., dinner 7–10 P.M.

City Rock Café (8)   112
Daily noon–2:30 A.M.

Fauchon (8)   113
Mon–Sat 8:30 A.M.–7 P.M.

Jacques Melac (11)   126
Mon–Fri bar and cold food, 9 A.M.–midnight, lunch
noon–3 P.M. Tues–Thur dinner, 7–10:30 P.M.

Jeremy's Sandwich & Coffee Shop (9)   122
Mon–Sat 9 A.M.–2 P.M.

Joe Allen (1)   37
Daily noon–1 A.M.

Juveniles (1)   38
Mon–Sat noon–11 P.M.

La Boutique à Sandwichs (8)   113
Mon–Sat 11:30 A.M.–1 A.M.

La Chocolatière (6)   89
Mon–Sat noon–7:30 P.M.

Ladurée (8)   114
Mon–Sat 8:30 A.M.–7 P.M., hot food 11:30 A.M.–3 P.M.

La Patata (2)   53
Daily 11 A.M.–midnight

L'Assiette aux Fromages (5)   77
Thur–Tues noon–11 P.M.

Le Café du Commerce (15)   132
Daily noon–midnight

L'Écluse (1, 6, 8, 11)   42, 93, 116, 128
Daily noon–1 A.M.

Le Cochon à l'Oreille (1)   42
Mon–Sat 4 A.M.–5 P.M.

Le Mouffetard (5)   80
Tues–Sat 7 A.M.–9 P.M., Sun 7 A.M.–4 P.M.

Le Roi du Pot-au-Feu (8)   117, 123
Mon–Sat noon–10 P.M.

Le Sancerre (7)   106
Mon–Fri 7:30 A.M.–8:30 P.M., Sat 8:30 A.M.–4 P.M.

Le Val d'Isère à Paris (8)   117
Daily noon–1:30 A.M.

Lina's Sandwiches (2, 8)   55, 118
Mon–Fri 9 A.M.–7 P.M. (2nd), Sat 9 A.M.–7 P.M. (8th)

Lunchtime (8)   118
Mon–Sat 11 A.M.–4 P.M.

Mariage Frères (4)   68, 95
Brunch Sat and Sun, noon–6 P.M., Lunch Tues–Sun,
noon–3 P.M., Tea Tues–Sun, 3–7 P.M.

Peny (8)   119
Daily breakfast, 7–11 A.M., lunch, noon–3 P.M., hot and
cold snacks 3–10 P.M.

Restaurant des Chauffeurs (16)   136
Daily noon–10 P.M.

Rose Thé (1)   47
Mon–Sat lunch, noon–5 P.M., tea 2:30–6 P.M.

San Francisco Muffin Company (4, 6)   70, 97
Daily 9 A.M.–8 P.M. (4th), Mon–Sat, 9 A.M.–8 P.M. (6th)

Tea Follies (9)   123
Mon–Sat 9 A.M.–9 P.M., Sun 9 A.M.–7 P.M.

RESTAURANTS OPEN IN AUGUST

The ever-growing number of tourists in Paris in
August has caused restauranteurs to begin keeping
their doors open during the once-sacred vacation
month of August. The following restaurants currently
state that they are open in August. It is important to
know that what a restaurant does one year may not be
the next year's policy, so to be sure, always call ahead.

RESTAURANTS OPEN ON SUNDAY

Rendez-Vous des Chauffeurs (18)   147
Restaurant Chez Marius (5)   83
Restaurant des Beaux Arts (6)   96
Restaurant des Chauffeurs (16)   136
Restaurant du Palais d'Orsay (7)   108
Restaurant le Petit Chose (18)   148
Tea Follies (9)   123
Trumilou (4)   70

GLOSSARY OF MENU AND FOOD TERMS

This glossary contains English explanations of the French menu terms used in this book as well as other common terms you are likely to encounter when dining out in Paris.

A

abricot	apricot
addition	restaurant bill
agneau	lamb
aiguillettes	thin slices, usually of duck breast
ail	garlic
aile	wing
aïoli	garlicky blend of eggs and oil
à la vapeur	steamed
à l'étouffée	stewed
aligot	pureed potatoes with melted Cantal cheese and garlic
allummettes	fried matchstick potatoes
amandes	almonds
ananas	pineapple
anchoïade	puree of anchovies, olive oil, and vinegar
andouille, andouillette	chitterlings (chitlins) sausage
aneth	dill
anguilles	eel
apéritif	before-meal drink
à point	medium rare
artichaut	artichoke
asperge	asparagus
assiette de	plate of
aubergine	eggplant
au four	baked
avocat	avocado

B

baguette	long thin loaf of bread
baies roses	pink peppercorns
ballotine	"small bundle," usually meat or fish, boned, stuffed, and rolled
banane	banana
bar	sea bass
barbue	brill
basilic	basil

basquaise	Basque style, with ham, sausage, tomatoes, and red pepper
bavarois	custard made with cream and gelatin
bavette	skirt steak
beignet	fritter, usually batter-fried fruit
Belon	flat-shelled oyster
betterave	beet
beurre	butter
bien cuit	well done
bifteck	steak (can be tough)
biologique	organic foods and wines
bisque	shellfish soup
blanc (de volaille)	breast (of chicken)
blanquette de veau	veal stew with onions, mushrooms, and cream
blette	Swiss chard
bleu	blood-rare (meat)
boeuf à la mode	beef marinated and braised in red wine
boeuf au gros sel	boiled beef with vegetables and coarse salt
boeuf bourguignon	beef cooked with red wine, onions, and mushrooms
boissons (compris ou non-compris)	drinks (included or not included)
boudin blanc	white sausage made with chicken or veal
boudin noir	pork sausage made with blood
bouillabaisse	Mediterranean fish and shellfish soup
bouilli	boiled
bourride	like bouillabaisse, but without shellfish
bouteille de	bottle of
braisé	braised
brochette	meat on a skewer
brûle	dark caramelization

C

cabillard	fresh cod
cacahouètes	peanuts
caille	quail
calamar	squid
canard	duck
caneton	young male duck
canette	young female duck
cannelle	cinnamon
carafe d'eau	pitcher of tap water
carbonnade	beef stew with onions and beer
carotte	carrot
carré d'agneau	rack of lamb
carte	menu
carte des vins	wine list

cassis	black currants
cassoulet	casserole of white beans with combinations of pork, duck, lamb, goose, and sausage
céleri rémoulade	shredded celery root salad with herbs and mayonnaise
cèpe	wild mushroom
cerise	cherry
cervelas	pork sausage with garlic; can also be fish or seafood sausage
cervelles	brains
champignon	mushroom
chanterelle	wild mushroom
Chantilly	sweetened whipped cream
charcuterie	cold cuts; *terrines*, pâtés, sausages; also a shop selling these and other deli items
charlotte	molded dessert, usually lined with ladyfingers
chaud	hot
Chavignin	sharp goat cheese
chèvre	goat cheese
chevreuil	venison
chicorée	curly endive
chiffonnade	thin strips, usually vegetables
chiperon	Basque word for squid
choix	choice
chou (rouge)	cabbage (red)
chou frisée	kale
choucroute	sauerkraut served with smoked meats
chou farci	stuffed cabbage
chou-fleur	cauliflower
choux	cream puff
choux de Bruxelles	Brussels sprouts
ciboulette	chive
cidre	apple cider
citron	lemon
citron vert	lime
civet de lièvre	stewed hare, thickened with blood
clafoutis	tarte of crêpe batter filled with fruit and baked; served warm
Claires	oysters
clementine	small Spanish tangerine
cochon	pig
cochonnailles	assortment of pork sausages and *pâtés* served as a first course
coeur	heart
coeur de filet	best part of beef fillet; chateaubriand
compote	stewed fruit

concombre	cucumber
confit	meat cooked and preserved in its own fat
confit d'oie	preserved goose
confiture	jam
contre-filet	cut of sirloin steak
coq-au-vin	mature chicken stewed in red wine
coquelet	young male chicken
coquillages	shellfish
coquilles St-Jacques	sea scallops
cornichon	tart pickle
côte	rib, chop
côte d'agneau	lamb chop
côte de boeuf	beef rib
côte de veau	veal chop
coulis	puree of raw or cooked vegetables or fruits
courge	squash
courgette	zucchini
couscous	granules of semolina; a spicy North African dish with semolina, various meats, and vegetables
couteau	knife
couvert	place setting
crème anglaise	custard sauce
crème brûlée	custard with a brown sugar glaze
crème caramel	custard with caramel flavoring
crème fraîche	fresh thick cream with the consistency of yogurt
crêpe	thin pancake
cresson	watercress
crevette grise	shrimp
crevette rose	prawn
croque-madame	toasted ham and cheese sandwich with an egg on top
croque-monsieur	toasted ham and cheese sandwich, no egg
(en) croûte	(in) a crust
crudités	raw vegetables
crustacés	shellfish
cuillère	spoon
cuisse de poulet	chicken leg
cuit	cooked
D	
datte	date
daube	meat stew
daurade	sea bream fish
déjeuner	lunch
dinde	turkey
dîner	dinner
duxelles	chopped mushrooms and shallots sautéed in butter and mixed with cream

E

eau (minérale)	water (mineral)
échalote	shallot
émincé	thin slice of meat
endive	chicory
entrecôte	beef rib steak
entrée	first course
épaule	shoulder of lamb, pork, etc.
épices	spices
épinard	spinach
escalope	thinly sliced meat or fish
escargot	snail
estouffade	beef stew
estragon	tarragon

F

façon	way of preparing a dish
faisan	pheasant
farci	stuffed
faux-filet	sirloin steak
fenouil	fennel
ferme	farm fresh
fermé	closed
(en) feuilleté	(in) puff pastry
fèves	broad beans
figue	fig
fines herbes	mixture of parsley, chives, and tarragon
flageolet	small, pale green kidney bean
flambé	flamed
flan	custard tart
flétan	halibut
fleur	flower
florentine	with spinach
foie	liver
foie de veau	calf's liver
foie de volaille	chicken liver
foie gras d'oie (canard)	goose liver (duck)
fond d'artichaut	heart and base of artichoke
fondue (du fromage)	melted (cheese)
forestière	garnish of wild mushrooms, bacon, and potatoes
(au) four	baked
fourchette	fork
fraîche, frais	fresh or chilled
fraise	strawberry
fraise des bois	wild strawberry
framboise	raspberry

fricassée	stewed or sautéed fish or meat
frisée	curly endive
frites (pommes)	French fries
froide	cold
fromage	cheese
fromage blanc	creamy cheese served for dessert with sugar
fruits de mer	seafood
fumé	smoked

G

galantine	boned meat, stuffed and glazed
galette	pancake, cake, or flat pastry
gambas	large prawns
garni	garnished
gâteau	cake
gâteau de riz	rice pudding
gaufre	waffle
gelée	aspic
génoise	sponge cake
gésier	gizzard
gibier	game
gigot (d'agneau)	leg (of lamb)
girofle	clove
girolles	wild mushrooms
glace	ice cream
glacé	iced, crystalized, or glazed
goujons	small catfish, breaded and fried
graine de moutard	mustard seed
gratin	crusty-topped dish or casserole
gratin dauphinois	scalloped potatoes
gratuit	free
(à la) grecque	cold vegetables cooked in a seasoned mixture of olive oil and lemon juice
grenouille (cuisses de)	frog (legs)
grillade	grilled
groseille	red currant
Gruyère	hard Swiss cheese

H

hachis	minced or chopped meat or fish
hareng	herring
haricot de mouton	mutton stew with white beans
haricot vert	green bean
homard	lobster
hor d'oeuvre	appetizer
huile	oil

huître	oyster

I

île flottante	poached meringue in custard sauce topped with caramel; used interchangeably with *oeufs à la neige*
infusion	herb tea

J

jambon	ham
jambon cru	salt-cured or smoked ham, aged but not cooked
jambonneau	pork knuckle
jardinière	garnish of fresh or cooked vegetables
jarret	shin
jeune	young
julienne	slivered vegetables
jus	juice

K

kir	aperitif made with *crème de cassis* and white wine
kir royale	*kir* made with champagne instead of wine

L

lait	milk
laitue	lettuce
langouste	small freshwater lobster (sometimes called crayfish)
langoustine	smaller than *langouste*
langue (de boeuf)	tongue (beef)
lapereau	young rabbit
lapin	rabbit
lardon	cubed, thick bacon
léger	light
légume	vegetable
lièvre	wild hare
lotte	large, firm-fleshed saltwater fish
loup de mer	similar to striped bass
lyonnaise (à la)	Lyon-style, usually with onions

M

mâche	lamb's lettuce
madeleine	small tea cake
magret de canard (oie)	breast of fattened duck (goose)
maigre	thin, no fat
maison (de la)	house (in the style of, or made there)
mandarine	tangerine
mange-tout	snow pea
maquereau	mackerel

marchand de vin	sauce with red wine, stock, and shallots
marché	market
marinée	marinated
marquise au chocolat	rich chocolate mousse cake
marron	chestnut
médaillon	round piece or slice
mélange	mixture
méli-mélo	assortment of fish served in a salad
menthe	mint
mer	sea
merguez	very spicy sausage
mesclun	mixture of seven types of baby salad greens
mets selon de la saison	according to the season
meunière	rolled in flour and cooked in butter
meurette	red wine sauce made with mushrooms, onions, bacon, and carrots
miel	honey
mignonette	small cubes of beef; coarsely ground white or black peppercorns
mille feuille	pastry with many layers, filled with pastry cream
mimosa	garnish of chopped hard-cooked egg
mirabelle	yellow plum
moelle	beef bone marrow
morceau	piece
morille	wild mushroom
morue	salted or dried cod fish
moule	mussel
mousse	light whipped mixture containing eggs and cream
mousseline	ingredients whipped with cream and eggs
moutarde	mustard
mouton	mutton
mûres	blackberries
myrtille	European blueberry
mystère	ice cream dessert; also meringue filled with ice cream and covered in chocolate sauce

N

nappé	covered with a sauce
nature	simple, plain, no sauce
navarin	lamb or mutton stew with root vegetables
navet	turnip
niçoise, à la	in the style of Nice; made with tomatoes, onions, anchovies, and olives
noisette	hazelnut; center cut of lamb chop; small rounds of potato
noix (de coco)	nuts (coconut)

normande	Normandy style, with cream and mushrooms or cooked in cider or Calvados
nouilles	noodles
nouvelle (cuisine)	new; describes foods in style of *nouvelle cuisine*: cooked with little butter or fat, artistically presented in small portions without heavy sauces

O

oeuf	egg
oeuf à la coque	soft-cooked egg
oeuf brouillé	scrambled egg
oeuf dur	hard-boiled egg
oeuf poché	poached egg
oeufs à la neige	whipped egg whites poached in milk; served in a custard sauce (used interchangeably with *île flottante*)
oie	goose
oignon	onion
onglet	beef cut similar to flank steak; can be strong tasting and tough
os	bone
oseille	sorrel
oursin	sea urchin
ouvert	open

P

pain	bread
pain Poilâne	round loaves of dark bread baked in wood-fired ovens
pamplemousse	grapefruit
panaché	denotes any mixture
pané	breaded
papillote	cooked in parchment paper
parfum	flavor
parmentier	dish with potatoes, usually mashed
pastis	anise liqueur
pâté	finely minced and seasoned meat, baked and served cold as a rich spread
pâté à choux	cream puff
pâtes (fraîche)	pasta (fresh)
pâtisserie	pastry
pavé	thick slice of meat
(à la) paysan	country style, with vegetables and bacon
pêche	peach
pêche Melba	peach with vanilla ice cream and raspberries
pêcheur	refers to fish preparations

perche	perch
perdreau	partridge
persil	parsley
petit déjeuner	breakfast
petit pain	roll
petit-pois	peas
petit salé (aux lentilles)	salted pork (with lentils)
pièce	a piece of something
pied (du porc)	foot (of pork)
pintade	guinea fowl
pipérade	Basque dish of scrambled eggs, pepper, ham, tomatoes, and onions
pistache	pistachio
pistou	sauce of basil, garlic, cheese, olive oil; sometimes stirred into fish soups
plat	dish
plat du jour	dish of the day
plateau de fruits de mer	platter of seafood
poêlé	pan-fried
poire	pear
poireau	leek
poire belle Hélène	poached pears with vanilla ice cream and hot chocolate sauce
poisson	fish
poitrine	breast of meat or poultry
poivre	pepper
poivron (rouge, vert)	pepper (red, green)
pomme	apple
pomme de terre	potato
pommes frites	French fries
porc (carré de, côte de)	pork (loin, chop)
potage	soup
pot-au-feu	beef simmered with vegetables
pot-de-crème	individual custard dessert
potée	rich soup with cabbage and pork
poularde	fatted hen
poulet (rôti)	chicken (roasted)
poulpe	octopus
pruneaux	prunes

Q

quenelle	dumpling, usually fish, veal, or poultry
quetsche	purple plum
quiche Lorraine	tart made with eggs, cream, ham, or bacon

R

racasse	saltwater fish
raclette	melted cheese on boiled potatoes, served with *cornichon* pickles and pickled onions
redis	radish
ragoût	stew
raie	skate fish (sting ray)
raisin	grape
râpé	grated or shredded
ratatouille	eggplant, zucchini, onions, tomatoes, and peppers, cooked with garlic and olive oil
rémoulade	sauce of mayonnaise, capers, mustard, herbs, and pickles
repas	meal
rillette	coarsely minced spread of duck, pork, and so on
ris (d'agneau, de veau)	sweetbreads (lamb, veal)
riz	rice
rognon	kidney
romarin	rosemary
rôti	roast
rouget	red mullet
roulade	rolled and stuffed meat or fish

S

sablé	shortbread-type cookie
safran	saffron
saignant	rare meat
saison (suivant la)	season (according to)
salade mixte	mixed salad
salade verte	green salad
salé	salted
sanglier	wild boar
sans alcool	without alcohol
saucisse	small fresh sausage
saucisson	large dried sausage
sauge	sage
saumon (fumé)	salmon (smoked)
sauté	browned in fat
savoyarde	flavored with Gruyère cheese
sel	salt
selle	saddle of meat
selon le marché	according to market availability
service compris	service charge included
serviette	napkin
sorbet	sherbet
soubise	onion sauce

sucre	sugar
suprême de volaille	chicken breast fillet

T

tapenade	puree of black olives, anchovies, capers, olive oil, and lemon juice
tarama	mullet roe made into a spread
tartare	chopped raw beef served with raw egg
tarte	open-faced pie
tarte Tatin	caramelized upside-down apple pie; served warm
tartine	buttered bread
tasse	cup
terrine	baked minced meat or fish; served cold
tête de veau	calf's head
thé	tea
thon	tuna
tiède	warm
tilleul	lime or linden blossom herb tea
tortue	turtle
tranche	slice
tripes à la mode de Caen	beef tripe, carrots, and onions cooked in cider and Calvados (apple brandy)
truite	trout

V

vacherin	dessert of baked meringue with ice cream and fresh cream
vapeur	steamed
veau	veal
velouté	veal or chicken cream sauce
verre	glass
viande	meat
volaille	poultry, fowl
vol au vent	flaky pastry shell

X

xérès	sherry

Y

yaourt	yogurt

READERS' COMMENTS

In *Cheap Eats in Paris*, I recommend places as they were at the time this book was printed and as I hope they will stay, but there are no guarantees. Every effort was made to ensure the accuracy of the information given, but prices, menu selections, opening and closing times, vacations, and ownership all can change overnight.

Cheap Eats in Paris is updated and revised on a regular basis. If you find a change before I do, or make an important discovery you want to pass along, please send me a note stating the name and address of the restaurant, the date of your visit and a description of your findings. Your comments are very important and I follow through on every letter sent. Thank you.

Send your comments to Sandra A. Gustafson (*Cheap Eats in Paris*), c/o Chronicle Books, 275 Fifth Street, San Francisco, CA 94103.

INDEX OF RESTAURANTS

Other travel guides by Sandra A. Gustafson:
Cheap Sleeps in Paris
Cheap Eats in London
Cheap Sleeps in London

Available in Spring 1993:
Cheap Eats in Italy
Cheap Sleeps in Italy

Available at your local bookstore. For a color catalog of all our books, call or write:

Chronicle Books
275 Fifth Street
San Francisco, CA 94103
1-800-722-6657